The Human Factor
At Work

A Guide To Self Reliance And Consumer
Protection For The Mind

Eric Oliver

MetaSystems
Canton, Michigan

Dedication

To my mentors: Joe, Joanne, Max Peter, Al,
John and Dave.

To Ian: For being there when I wasn't.

To Tess: For being there when I was.

Acknowledgements

First and last I thank my wife Tess for creating the environment within which this book could be written. Next, my great thanks to Dr. Larry Dossey for taking time to read and comment on my work in the introduction. My erstwhile agent Sarah Jane Freyman charted the course the final book took; my father, Joe Oliver, as well as Tom and Marlene Denney and Mack Ed Swindle kept the project from foundering forever; my friends Charles Faulkner, Ian Oliver and Vern Holmberg kept the ideas true to their roots, and my mentors Al Lipp, Dr. John Grinder and Dr. Dave Dobson planted and nurtured most of these ideas.

In addition to my debt to these people, a large share of thanks goes to my former clients and students, who offered me their opinions about the value of my work in their professional and personal lives. Among them, I would be remiss if I failed to single out Beth Allard, Al Wadleigh, Denny Martel, John Carey, and Barb Jones for their various individual gifts which created the climate in which that flow of information could be passed and helped me scratch out the footprints remembered here in ink.

All this would be academic were it not for Thorn and Ursula Bacon, my originally bewildered—but later determined—editors, who took the fruits of 15 years work honing non-verbal communication which—on paper—was completely unintelligible and made sense—in print—of it.

"Nothing worth doing
Can be achieved in our lifetime;
Therefore we must be saved by hope.
Nothing which is true or beautiful or good
Makes complete sense in any immediate
Context of history;
Therefore we must be saved by faith.
Nothing we do, however virtuous,
Can be accomplished alone;
Therefore we must be saved by love."

Reinhold Niebuhr

"There is no answer.
There never has been an answer.
There never will be an answer.
That's the answer."

Gertrude Stein

Introduction

For two centuries, modern medicine has been searching for magic bullets—powerful drugs or surgical procedures that can be applied to all humans, in identical fashion, to solve problems. This questionable way of thinking has invaded modern psychology and psychiatry as well. Everyone is looking for *The Formula*, the magic bullet, for every disordered emotion and human failing. In the New Age, this frequently involves a search for the correct thought, attitude or set of emotions.

This approach neglects the obvious: People are different. The working of the psyche, the habits and the overall mental makeup of one individual are unlike that of any other. Because we are utterly unique, there is no hope, even in principle, that we can discover some formula that can be applied to everyone in hopes of solving any problem whatsoever.

In *The Human Factor At Work,* Eric Oliver cuts like a laser beam through all the current hype about formulaic approaches and magic bullets to solving problems. He asks us to go past the easy answers that always fall short and disappoint. He asks us to focus on what makes us unique individuals, and he provides specific guidelines about how to enrich and empower our lives through relating and communicating more effectively with others.

There is a tendency in psychology to ruminate on the past and to explore endlessly why we are the way we are. This book has a different starting point. Given our weaknesses and strengths, our habits both good and bad, what steps can we take to strengthen and enrich our lives? Readers should understand that these issues are not "just psychology." People who relate effectively to others and who have rich and gratifying social contacts, are healthier and live longer than people whose lives are socially constricted and who don't know how to get on with others. That is why Eric Oliver's book is good medicine as well as good psychology, and why I am delighted to recommend it.

Larry Dossey, M.D.

Author: *Healing Words*
Meaning & Medicine
Recovering The Soul
Space, Time & Medicine

Table Of Contents

1

False Advertising And Protection

The *Human Factor At Work* rests on the observation that personal success relies on your skill at getting along with other people. And you'll learn how to do it better in this book. All of us know in our hearts that success in life is almost entirely dependent upon our associations with others around us. This book asks readers to start putting more "us" back in "U.S." and take out the more self-centered and less effective "me."

Somewhere along the way in our pursuit of happiness, we seem to have lost sight of the fact that "happiness" comes about from getting things done. We've trained ourselves to spend too much time trying to unearth the causes of human problems and plan solutions for them. We've left ourselves little if no time to act!

Because we are creatures of habit and not of specific intention, this has not been a helpful path to follow. It is not healthful, it is not natural, and it hasn't worked. We are not like our automobiles, able to be tuned up, fueled, and guided by a map to a predetermined destination down roads which go only where we expect them to. We are, as St. Teresa said, "… like a wild horse; perfectly willing to go anywhere except where you try to point it."

The direction this book points to may help you to give up trying to predict the outcome of human situations and trying to consciously manage each step of your way to personal happiness.

The people I work with who have learned to do this are more pleased with themselves and more successful in their careers. And they have discovered how to understand and work better with others. Those are valuable benefits.

In a country founded on the philosophy of independence, the minds of all Americans certainly ought to be safe from intrusive influence. Most of us do in fact live as if mental safety were a fundamental right. But few of us have learned to protect the part of ourselves we call the mind from ideas that may seem beneficial, but turn out to be harmful to the development of our full potential.

Without thinking much about it we've assumed that our minds are safe, and we act much like the farmer who assumed the stock in the barn was free from harm. By the time we notice a threat and race to lock the barn door, it's usually too late.

For centuries people wondered how their minds worked. As we learned and practiced the Scientific Method, we began pretending that the secrets of the mind undoubtedly would show up under a microscope any minute. Since the beginning of the century we profited by selling speculations on how the mind works. These notions have been treated like a commodity and we have created a brisk business with answers to questions about the mind. Advertising for mind commodities has penetrated education, parenting, business, politics and the media.

As a result, a whole industry of mind evaluation, diagnosis and instruction has risen in which prescribed thinking has been substituted for actions. Since the end of World War I, Americans have bought and sold linguistic fictions such as "Positive Attitudes." We've done this at the expense of our capacity to improve our chances of relating to one another directly.

Human beings live mainly by habit, not by good intention. We act first, and think later. By overvaluing labels and mental recipes for success we've sold ourselves an illusion of control we really don't have. We've been buying the notion that "taking charge of our lives" is as simple as purchasing some empowerment or self-esteem or assertiveness.

The Human Factor At Work demonstrates that this habit of buying and selling fictional active ingredients for the mind as the simple easy solution to human problems has actually made things worse. That is because human problems are solved in the real world in the company of other people—not inside our heads! What I hope to do in this book is to provide you with practical skills for improved interaction with other people, to use both professionally and personally.

We are all prepared to consider how we might protect the environment, our businesses, our families and our social structures. However, few of us consider how little we do to protect and enhance that part of our mind which directs all our efforts. We don't look after our minds very well. Fortunately, an extensive education isn't necessary. All you need is some on-the-job training. You'll find that here in this book.

Before we discuss how to protect the mind, let's decide what it is and what it does. First, the mind is *not* your brain. According to the experts who've spent the last generation trying to locate the mind, its functions are turning up all over your body. And if you take into account the fact that the mind's functions have a lot to do with electricity inside and outside your body, it becomes even more difficult to pin down.

Also, the mind isn't just the part you are using to read and make sense of these words, right now. The mind is much more than that. The part of our awareness we use when we talk to ourselves to reflect on our daily lives is just about the *smallest part* of the mind there is!

The major portion of the mind is the part we rely on to *do* things; it is also the part we rely on to *notice* what we've done; and finally, it is the part which supplies us with the words to discuss those things—*after the fact.*

This is where wise consumers begin to pay closer attention. The mind is not the part of the brain which speaks to itself about what you may want, what you have done, or how you feel about things. You can prove this. Think of a word—any word. Obviously, you didn't know what the word would be before you thought of it, did you? But some part of you selected the word. That part didn't wait to be told what to do.

The part of your mind that tries to tell you things—your conscious mind—depends entirely for each word you use upon the part of your mind *outside* consciousness to find that word. The truth is, nobody can tell us exactly what the mind is, but the experts do know a lot about how it works. And much of what we've been taught about how to use our minds in our professional and personal lives is reversed from what those experts know about it now. We didn't learn how to use our minds in special schools; it happened in the real, day-to-day world of jobs, and television, and attitude-adjustment-hours after work. Also, the teaching hasn't stopped. It's happening, as Alan Funt used to say, "When you least expect it!"

How does the mind work?

It works just like you've heard, habitually—from habit. We're all creatures of habit.

The last time you got off an elevator at the wrong floor just by following the crowd of other people, you caught yourself involved in a habitual function. Would it surprise you to know that more than 90% of your daily life works just exactly that same way?

The inner workings of the mind are still pretty complicated stuff, but the fact to remember is that the mind works by <u>habit</u>. Its main function, beyond keeping us alive, is to build and maintain the thousands of habits we use to move through the world every day without thinking about them.

We have habits for everything from our morning routine in the bathroom, to how we react to being harshly criticized. Virtually all of what we do on a day-to-day basis is the function of the learned habits of thinking and acting we've had for years.

Most of us, at one time or another, have noticed the habits we've developed to maintain our bodies: how we get dressed, one pant leg at a time, how we eat soup, how we walk, the way we go to sleep, and so on. Some of us also have noticed the habits we exhibit in our interactions with other people: how we greet everyone in the office each morning, how we drive, how we answer the phone, how we plan our week, how we criticize and how we offer compliments. Few of us have taken the time to notice that what most would call the more "important" parts of daily life are just as habitual as the others.

These "more important" habits of thought and action are the parts of the mind that will benefit the most from a little protection. To whom we are attracted is decided in the same habitual, unthinking way as how we tie our shoes. We know when to say "no" to an idea by using the same kind of habits we use to remember phone numbers. We know when to laugh at a joke because of the same kind of habits that remind us that we don't like strawberries. We know how to act confident, or lonely, or aggressive through the same kind of habitual thinking that allows us to recognize someone from a distance, even if she turns out not to be the person we thought she was.

Where do these habits start?

The answer to this question may surprise you. When somebody does something of which you strongly disapprove, or surprises you in an unpleasant way, what is the first question you are likely to ask him? If your answer is: "*Why* did you do that?" bear in mind that he probably never questioned his actions in that way. Our emotional, mental and behavioral habits do not begin with a strong intention or a good reason, and then become incorporated into our actions. Instead, your mind (outside consciousness) years ago selected several specific responses to the world and began automatically displaying them in given situations. If the selected responses were reinforced at the time they were displayed, then it is likely they would emerge even stronger in a similar situation in the future. Continued reinforcement would encourage the mind to respond in the same fashion in other related or similar situations.

An easy example is smoking. A person who is just about to light his first cigarette has a rough idea about some of the things on his mind. But not all those things. How could he? There are a minimum of 200,000,000 things going on in your mind every second, while your conscious, evaluating part has only *seven* bits of information to work with.

If the person continues to smoke for a month, the mind will have automated the entire procedure of fetching, lighting and smoking cigarettes to the point that the smoker can smoke an entire pack without any conscious awareness of it at all, until he pulls the last one from the pack. At that point, he may get mad at people who bum smokes from him, thinking he gave all of his cigarettes away! The process of smoking is so unthinking that the smoker can accidentally light the wrong end of a cigarette, or light a second while the first is still going.

By the time a month has passed, the question, "Why are you smoking that cigarette?" has become irrelevant. The smoker's mind has by that time translated the actions and sensations of the smoking habit to respond to cues from hundreds, even thousands, of incentive situations, thoughts or moods. The smoker is entirely unconscious of the process. He may even find himself reaching for a cigarette without realizing his desire was triggered by the sound of someone striking a match behind him. Habits have no "whys" behind them and we are—as you know—creatures of habit.

What holds true for smoking is equally accurate for the habits involved in choosing the type of person who attracts you, how you approach a tough job, how you react to success or failure, and how you know when to quit. Your emotional, mental and behavioral habits start outside conscious awareness, are cued to happen outside conscious awareness, and are reinforced or diminished outside consciousness. Reasons, or the answer to the question, "Why did I do that?" are merely conscious editorials about the process.

Does this mean my mind is always on automatic pilot?

No. Just more than 90 percent of the time. It works in a certain order. Functions outside consciousness happen first, then if your action is consciously noted, you may reflect on what you have done. We form impressions or gut feelings about the world, act on them, and *then* decide why we did so. The habitual formula is, "Ready, go ... set!"

Think of the last time you met several new and different

people. How quickly did you form impressions about each one? Which ones were more interesting and which were less? Which ones were attractive, and which ones weren't? Which ones did you feel more—or less—comfortable near? Which ones would you rather work with? Now, carefully go back over the order in which things occurred and you will discover something valuable about how you might work with your mind respective of the way it really functions. Notice that today you can come up with plenty of answers to the question, "Why did I feel that way about so-and-so?" But at the time you experienced the feeling you formed an inside impression, and *then* you came up with an explanation for that impression.

Outside consciousness first, then inside. It only becomes totally autopilot if you quit paying attention consciously to the process. Unfortunately, that's exactly what we've all been asked to do. Lacking any protection from those messages in our surroundings, most of us act in ways which abdicate our responsibility to pay attention to the process of living. Implicitly and explicitly, we have promoted the idea that the process doesn't start until the "why" question is asked and answered. In the real, day-to-day world, that's the last step.

How does this kind of false advertising take place?

In every field of human endeavor, we've extolled the idea that the important stuff doesn't begin until we start discussing reasons why somebody did, said or felt something. In the real world, we creatures of habit are just about finished doing, saying or feeling whatever it may be by the time our conscious mind catches up and begins speculating why that may have occurred.

In business we've learned to seek one management "why" after another. "Effective Listening," "Management by Results," and "Total Quality Incentives" are examples of ideas for easily explained, easily written *answers*. The solutions we've accepted are all simple; they have an outline, and usually at least seven steps. They are specifically aimed at specific targets.

This bull's-eye imagery is designed to magnify the importance of "why" we're aiming at whatever it is we're aiming at.

In the personal growth field, it's the same kind of thing. First we're encouraged to discuss exactly why we aren't getting what we want out of life. Then, we're told we need a specific outline (seven steps again) with specific understandings to be reached, specific steps to take, and an easily targeted and specific goal to aim for.

The commodity being sold is essentially an answer to the question "why"—which comes last, not first, in your reactions to life. Whether the answer you dream up is positive or negative really doesn't matter, if phrasing follows function as it actually seems to do.

Well, if stopping to ask "why" doesn't help, what will?

I like to think of the mind's functions like a train; the train of thought and action. What seems to work to get my clients to act in more brain-friendly ways for themselves, and among others, is to remember the order in which the mind works rather than trying to ignore part of that function in favor of the parts we can more easily sit back and discuss consciously.

The problem with this habit of thinking is that it can limit our chances of succeeding in what we wish to accomplish both at home and at work. Your mind doesn't stop to say, "Here's why you should light a cigarette now," nor does it do the same with any other professional or personal habits.

Think of words, and conscious discussion as the Caboose on your train of thought. The Caboose doesn't pull the Train, nor can it push it. A word pops into your head, then you notice it consciously, and finally you begin making up reasons for having come up with that particular word. That reason-making process is the Caboose.

The passenger and freight cars on your train of thought are made up of all those habits for thinking and action we build and reinforce outside consciousness to get through life. Most of us have been encouraged to assume that our thinking is an orderly, rational and verbal process. Self-talk. Thinking is not just talking to yourself. Lots of these habits have no verbal components at all.

If you identify a spot on the track of life, the cars on your train of thought composed of habits of thinking and action will always pass over that spot before the Caboose will. You feel, act or respond to something, then you can talk about it—bringing up the Caboose.

The Engine on your train of thought is your ability to feel a certain type of sensation. It's always expressed somewhere along the midline of your body, either as an awkward or fearful sensation, or as the opposite—a relaxed in-control, secure sensation.

When we react in the world, we do so by first enacting a cue from the engine in our train of thought—outside consciousness—which leads to a habitual response of thought and behavior: the cars. The cars are followed last by the option of noticing and consciously remarking on our response: the Caboose. Notice that conscious self-talk doesn't even arise until almost the whole train of thought and action has already passed on.

If I didn't talk my way into my habits for a reason, then how did I learn them?

You learned how to be yourself from the way you've acted with others. And, despite almost a century of successful sales of simple, easy solutions to consumers of ideas about the mind, we still don't do things for particular reasons—we do things, and then make up reasons for having done them. You learned to act the way you do by processing examples from the people around you. You perceive of yourself in light of those habits as you look back over your life so far. To improve your pursuit of happiness, you might wish to notice and direct the most fundamental part of your mind's functions; its constant responsiveness to the actions and suggestions of others. We all know that, much as we sometimes hate to admit it, people work more on the principle of "Monkey See, Monkey Do" than of "Monkey Understand, Monkey Do."

Stop and think of an example of success. Now think of a failure. Think of a success you haven't had yet. Ditto for a failure. With my clients, I go through each example until it becomes clear to all concerned that whatever "success and failure" are to you, they are *both* directly or at least indirectly dependent on the contributions and actions of other people besides yourself. The habits you now own came from modeling without understanding bits and pieces of the habits of parents, teachers, ministers, and TV stars.

What's wrong with trying to understand life and changing myself for the better?

Trying to understand life interferes with living it. But the real answer to this question is that we must overcome the belief that changes in human relations start from inside the individual.

One of the most common analogies used to sell that notion is the one about peeling an onion. You are asked to envision the difficulties in your life today as if they were the outer layers of an onion. Your job is to pull off one layer at a time and investigate the "whys" underlying each successive layer. That is supposed to lead to a new understanding and, of course, to a simple, easy way to take control of your life from that point on. You're told that once you've accomplished this, your relations with others can only improve.

Try the onion trick with a real onion and see what you end up with. There is <u>no</u> center to be uncovered. An onion is an accumulation of hundreds of leaves pressed together. If you try to take them apart to find the "real" onion inside, all you get is a handful of leaves and a lot of tears. Very much like what we've gotten for years trying to take apart our lives by conscious, verbal means—attempting to improve ourselves in ways that aren't very brain-friendly and don't respect the way your train of thought runs.

In our zeal to buy and sell the illusion of control, we forgot how we learned our habits in the first place. Notice that the focus, whether in Personal Growth or Professional Development, is still on the Caboose for both the source of every problem and the prescriptions for success. All of the mental improvement programs sell "whys" for what ails you, and "whys" for how you should fix it. All the effort starts inside the head of the consumer, as if finding the right vocabulary will force the world outside your Caboose to adjust to you.

You learn your habits of thinking and acting from interactions with other people, not from listing pros and cons in your own head. You learned your beliefs, biases and emotional responses the way you learned to ride in elevators, to walk, or to speak English. The process happens with some conscious direction, but not by conscious means. None of us talk our way into our reactions as much as we form habits for acting certain ways, and then talk about them. For decades the Baptists have said, "You can't think your way into better living; you can only live your way into better thinking."

Consumer protection becomes critical when you appreciate that the attempt to postpone your life long enough to try to put it into words usually hurts more than it helps.

What about the importance of setting goals? That has to

be expressed in words, doesn't it?

This outcome-oriented, goal-line habit of thinking is actually a fairly new approach. Its popularity can be attributed much more to the ease with which it can be packaged than to any tried-and-true effectiveness it actually has in real life. Real life doesn't work this way and we all know it. When was the last time you set out to accomplish something that involved the contributions and efforts of several other people, and that ended up working out precisely the way you imagined it would, every step of the way? Was it school? Your first job? Marriage? How about raising children? Has this approach *ever* worked for you?

Much of what we currently buy in terms of goal-setting and self-control is shoddy merchandise. Humans act first, think later, and learn from the reinforcement of those experiences. Can you begin to appreciate the advantages of getting more and more involved interacting with other human beings instead of just planning to in your head? Goals usually just limit you.

I saw a photograph of a football player taken on press day the week before the Super Bowl. On this day all the players for both teams suit up without pads and make themselves available to the assembled world press corps for questions. Because the only event which garners more press than the Super Bowl is a war, there are almost always enough reporters present so that even the second string long-snapper gets interviewed.

The photo I referred to shows a football player arrayed in his uniform behind his banner, with more press within reach than he would ever have available at one time again. And what is he doing? Is he greeting them? Joking with them? Discussing his game strategy? Before I answer that question, remember that all players want enough press to increase their notoriety. After their four or five gridiron years are over, they want to be remembered so that the car dealership or bar they buy will benefit from their fame. Their livelihood depends on getting noticed and making the most of it. So, it's no surprise for us to find out that many of the smarter players work hard at learning methods of presenting themselves in powerfully productive ways.

But the player in the photo was sitting alone, surrounded by the people who could help *make* his future. Apparently, he wasn't quite finished setting goals, motivating himself and planning his communication strategy. He was making sure he understood exactly the right way to influence all those press people. He was sitting with his head down in a book, which was instructing him on the seven powerful ways he could act effectively with those people all around him—some other day, soon.

What good are words then, if everything's just habit?

If we put them to their proper use, instead of trying to pull our Trains around behind the Caboose, words can provide more and more valuable directions for us to take. All we have to give up is the illusion that we can accurately predict and control the outcomes of other people. Since simple experiences, like raising children or managing offices, provide ample evidence which contradicts the idea of control, there's really not much to give up after all.

The illusion of control by conscious means demands a world in which everything can be separated, labeled and *controlled* within your own head. Brain-friendly approaches, however, are those which acknowledge that the mind outside consciousness will respond quite well to direction, but poorly to dictation. Remember, this is because the mind works with impressions of experiences before explanations and the majority of our important thinking comes not only nonverbally, but outside conscious reach. We have the opportunity to direct our learning and our performance more productively if we use *all* parts of the Train of Thought in the order in which they apparently work the best.

How do I start noticing which messages I want to follow, and how do I direct my mind instead of dictating to it?
In the following chapters you'll encounter different methods of handling Words, Thinking, and especially Feelings in interactions with other people.

The exercises are designed to help you take advantage of your greatest asset: the people around you, and your ability to form and maintain new habits of your own based on the time spent with these people. There are really only two requirements to meet. First, you'll want to pay more attention to what other people are doing each day. Secondly, you'll want to occasionally practice acting a bit differently *before* you think about why you are doing it.

Too many of us have bought into the promise that we can change ourselves the way we change our socks. We can't control our minds any more than we can "manage time." People who run the better time management courses are the first to point out that you can't really manage time. You can't give yourself a minute, grab a couple of seconds or spend an hour you don't have. The day is 24 hours. What we can begin to manage differently is what we actually do during the moments of the day.

When it comes to achieving greater success with our habits of thinking and acting, the same holds true. You can't manage your*self,* but you can often direct what you *do* with yourself. My favorite oxymoron is "self-control."

A friend of mine once said, "If you're sitting on a fence, lean in the direction you want to fall." Words lean us in one direction or the other, and our hidden thinking habits lean us toward predetermined reactions to events even more than the words. That thinking is advertised in our demeanor whether we know it or not. We respond more directly to advertising in demeanor and behavior than we do to language. As you know, it's not *what* is said, it's *how.* You are who you are today by virtue of learning how to react to that kind of advertising from signals you receive and reinforce, not from internal dialogues with yourself. True self-reliance comes much more from constructive interactions with others than it does from attention to ourselves and our inner editorials.

o   o   o

You can't control yourself by conscious means because the Train of Thought and Action runs habitually.

2

Words, Meaning and the Mind

People are primates first and high school graduates second. Although we often act as if the reverse were true, it isn't. Other primates don't have a spoken language, but they still manage to get their business done among themselves. So do we, and our talent for language has allowed us to spread our business far—as far as the moon.

Such accomplishments often cause us to lose sight of the fact that we still do a lot of things the same way other primates do. These actions include the mannerisms we use to emphasize our spoken words. Often, what's said between people only exaggerates those signals our body has already conveyed. However, our talent for language which enabled us to perform great technical accomplishments has a down side.

The down side is that language can distract us from attending to one another to the point of hampering our interactions and chances for long-term success.

Often, when I do training, my first exercise is to ask people to close their eyes and think of an ocean for a few moments. Now, I want you to imagine such a body of water. The picture that comes up in your mind's eye will never be the same as that of another person. Some people remember a time they visited an ocean, others flash on pictures of oceans from movies, books, magazines or paintings.

Whatever the response, there are four things you can now appreciate about that ocean in your head.

1. It isn't the only ocean in your head. If you stop to think about it you can start imagining or remembering all sorts of other ocean scenes in addition to the first one. Your head is filled with thousands of images, sounds, descriptions and actual experiences of different oceans. You've been storing these oceans in your mind before you even knew the word "ocean".

2. Your ocean refuses to stay the same; it changes from moment-to-moment as you concentrate on it. Your mind is powerful and it works at an incredible rate sorting through vast amounts of information and experience before letting some of it through for you to talk about. If you concentrate on your ocean for a few seconds, you'll notice details—the coming or going of waves, smells or tastes, colors and shapes. Many of you will even discover totally different oceans, popping into your mind unbidden. The search-and-retrieval function of your mind and language is called *transderivational processing*. You can't stop it.

Try spending 60 seconds concentrating on one ocean in your head, with no change. It would be just as hard to try to go back to your very first image of an ocean and try to retrieve it. Precisely.

3. Your ocean is unlike anybody else's in the whole world. You have a unique set of experiences in your mind, having accumulated and stored them all of your life. No two people have the same experiences, because no two people share the same brain,

body or history. Even identical twins have different impressions of the world and vastly different reactions to it. Of all the thousands of oceans floating around in your head, all are different from anybody else's.

4. You can't think of just one ocean. You may only have one in your conscious attention at the moment, but it came from the same place in your mind that delivered all the others. By focusing on the idea of ocean, and upon the reference ocean you came up with, your mind began searching and your imagination went to work.

You have multiple oceans in your head. They are always changing. How can you use these facts about oceans, about your mind's treatment of language through transderivational processing to both protect yourself and improve your chances of success in life?

One answer is that if everybody has multiple references for the word "ocean," then obviously we have multiple references for the other words we use as well. When it's just "ocean," it's an interesting feature of your brain's functioning. But what happens when you pick another word?

For instance, have you ever been walking down a hallway at the office early in the morning and were feeling just fine? Suddenly, a coworker stops you with a concerned look on her face and asks seriously, "Are you sick?"

If you've ever had this happen, you know what usually comes next. Your brow wrinkles as you try to guess what prompted her concern and you say something like, "No, I don't think so. Why? Do I look sick? Maybe I'm coming down with something. I was a little tired yesterday."

How many references for "sick" do you imagine popped up behind the curtain of consciousness and began exerting their influence on your state of mind and body the whole time you kept your conscious attention on that word "sick?"

How differently do you think things would have turned out if you had replied, "No, I'm feeling particularly well today. Do I look un-*well*?"

"Well" is a lot more fun than "sick"—especially since this word immediately triggers several thousand other "well" images in the storage of your mind.

How about the word "priority"? What if you heard: "Our priorities are totally out of line?" Or what if you told someone: "I want you to make this your top priority," even though she already has three other "top priorities" in her head from last month? What does it mean to us when we hear it from either our boss or a co-worker? We know that the way we associate words with our experiences gives them a real and personal meaning. These meanings are not static but are constantly changing and unique to each set of ears. Appreciating this fact can help us on our road to success.

Have your associations for the word "love" stayed the same over the last five years? And if you "love" someone in particular, how quickly does that word change its meaning and reference in your head over the period you actually spend time with that person? We can learn a lot more about each other if we treat written words as the only part of our interactions with others that stay the same. Everything else—from our associations with those words to our feelings prompted by those associations—is constantly shifting in our heads.

What about the third observation that everybody's "ocean" is different from everybody else's? How can that help in real life? Stop and think for a second. If you remember that everyone has unique associations in his mind for the words he uses, would you be more or less likely to get hopping mad if somebody used the "wrong" word with you?

In my consulting work I've run across many instances of people coming close to blows over this discrepancy between mental worlds. One person knows what "control" is, but another can't see it. This one wants more "discipline" while that one thinks "discipline" is overrated. "Empowerment is a must for every one of our people," the boss says, while everybody listening thinks about how little "power" they themselves possess. Have you ever heard an argument start with one of the following statements: "Well, I love you more than you love me" or "You have no self-esteem" or "Why are you always so unreasonable?" or "I can't take your ambition any longer?"

Not long ago I received a phone call from Bob, the personnel director of a large utility company. Even though we hadn't been in touch with each other for several years, it took him but a moment to outline the problem for which he wanted my help. It illustrates the idea of discrepancies between how people perceive the meaning of words that accompany actions.

It seems that one of the company's quality control managers had been driving everyone to distraction. No one wanted to work with him any longer, but Bob thought the man was valuable because of his expertise. He was described as arrogant, blunt and unresponsive. A mile-long list of complaints had been lodged against him because of his use of an exaggerated technical vocabulary. He drowned his listeners with erudite words, then often would leave without waiting to see if his comments and requests had been understood.

Bob asked me how long it would take me to "fix" Fred's communication problem.

"Either two days, or never," I replied without hesitation. Bob responded with a hearty, "For that, you're hired."

Some people pick up the irritating habit—probably just before and during early school days—of acting smart. Some people outgrow it, others manage to bring it into adulthood and use it in a variety of situations—from interactions with people at work, friends at play and with their families at home.

Some people believe irritating behavior is nothing more than a case of a poor attitude that needs to be adjusted by a professional. The staff of the personnel department at the utility company was no exception, and labeled Fred as one with an "attitude problem."

Within a day of my return home from visiting with Fred the personnel director called me before I had a chance to submit my report. Bob sounded breathless as he rushed to tell me about the wave of surprise washing through the corporate hallways concerning the miraculous change in Fred's attitude. It was noticed all the way to the big boss.

The only two people who knew there was no real change in this man's attitude were Fred and I. Working with Fred had not been difficult. After getting acquainted with him, I asked him only one critical question, "Would you rather be right, or employed?"

His answer was sincere—of course, he wanted to keep his job. As I worked with him, we practiced the two things he would have to do differently if he wanted to keep his job, and neither one had anything to do with attitude, nor was his motivation an issue.

The first thing I instructed him to do was how to sit or stand when greeting a person to make the individual feel welcomed and the target of attention. (See Chapters XI and XII). Respecting the mind's habit of "monkey see" over "monkey understand" when it comes to action, we practiced this for most of two days at a local mall.

The second thing I suggested was that Fred become aware of the unique and specific terms people at work used in their conversations and told him to start substituting these words for his own favorite expressions in all future correspondence with these individuals, as well as in his conversations with them. Fred thought for only a moment and was quick to remember pet phrases and words his co-workers used freely.

He made a conscientious effort to immediately apply my simple directions in his communications with his co-workers, who naturally concluded a miracle had occurred.

If you speak—particularly in important situations—as if everybody has the same associations for every "ocean" you have, you are likely to get unpleasant reactions as Fred had. Think about words like "fair, honest, mean, aggressive, dependent, irresponsible, powerful, strong," and you begin to recognize the truth that there's a lot more going on in human interactions than meets the ear.

Imagine that you went to see a psychotherapist because you'd been feeling blue for a while and you were ready to start back on the road you want to travel. Would the following—correct and professional—set of questions help or hurt you? Remember, the brain works at 200,000,000 bits per second and it never sleeps. And, for every word you hear, a part of your mind is instantly busy collecting and pushing forward—towards consciousness—every associated experience you've ever had with that word.

Question: "How long have you been depressed?"
Answer: "Oh, it's hard to say."
Question: "Have you ever been depressed before?"
Answer: "Not exactly like this."
Question: "Are you more depressed at night, or during the day?"
Answer: "It's sort of even. But mostly during the day."
Question: "Was your mother depressed? Was your father

depressed? Do you work among people who are depressed? Have you ever been hospitalized or treated for depression before? Have other people told you you are depressed? How do you exhibit this depression? Are you depressed going to sleep? Do you wake up depressed? Do you eat when you're depressed?" Quick! How do you feel? Happy-go-lucky? Depressing, isn't it? The word isn't magic, and it certainly can't *make* you depressed. But you sure can appreciate how words can make things more or less vivid.

This occurs due to our mind's ability to reinforce with memories whatever words we bring to its attention. We can't just talk ourselves into health or sickness, but the way our mind processes talk is definitely going to help or hinder the outcome.

The words you process in your mind are not neutral. There is no safety zone between your ears—where it's safe to drone on for four hours about a "problem"—without reinforcing that very thing of which you speak.

If you wish to take full advantage of your experience with the "ocean" exercise, it is helpful to begin acting among other people in concert with what you learned from it.

First, don't assume that anyone else on the planet has the same things associated with a word that you do. One person's meat truly *is* another's poison. If you presume in both your speech and actions that everyone around you is responding to the experiences in *your* head, you are guaranteed to find yourself often surprised and frequently misunderstood. You may frequently find yourself alone.

Second, give up the idea that you can *predict* what association someone else might have connected with a word in his head. I once asked a group to think of an "ocean" and as I went about asking what people had come up with, one person said, "cranberries."

That stopped me dead in my tracks for a second until I saw the *Oceanspray Cranberry* juice bottle sitting by his side.

Remember those cranberries the next time you order somebody to do something "better" or "quickly" or "now" or "faster" or "properly" or "right" or "clearly" or "by tomorrow" or "like last time" or "efficiently" or "cheaper" or "the best you can." Stop for a second, breathe deeply, and as you sigh, remember everybody has a different "ocean" in their head.

Third, stop acting as if your "ocean" is the best one. The only person your "ocean" (or "attitude" or "motivation" or "self-esteem") is best for is you. Use some care when you are communicating. If you discover in the course of conversation with somebody that he has a much less pleasant associations for a word than you do, give up that word when you're with him.

I've told the therapists I've worked with: "If you *know* your client suffers from post-traumatic stress disorder, but she insists on calling it 'radish,' then by all means, you call it 'radish,' too. But only once, while you find a *third* word which isn't associated with anything so evocative for either of you."

If you are in sales and you aren't asking your customer what she wants from a product or service if she could have everything she wished, then mentally tally up her "oceans" and use those key words to describe your product/service—please start doing it. It works!

Even if your company's marketing team spent thousands of dollars designing brochures with very special, important (magical) words to describe the features and benefits your company offers, the problem is that your customer has different features and benefits in her mind . Those words on the paper are only magic for the brains that put them on the paper. For other people, they may be excess stomach acid.

It is most constructive for parents and managers to act as if people were actually speaking an unfamiliar language to them. If you assume the other person really *doesn't* understand what you're saying, you might pay attention to the way you can direct and communicate with him more effectively. That means, like Fred, you would respect that actions really *do* speak loudest.

Fourth, quit correcting other peoples' words for them. They are already correct. If you can possibly do it, make every effort to use their words. If you can't do that, change the words in your speech which are offensive to them. Steer clear of telling them outright that their words are wrong. That is, unless you truly want to be rid of that person. If you want her out of your life, take every opportunity to correct her language and she'll soon run screaming away from you tearing her hair out as she goes.

Fifth, please remember how words can reinforce the outcome of any given situation even though they can't control it. There are no hypothetical situations for your mind. *The mind makes no distinction outside consciousness between what's vividly imagined and what's actually real.* Whatever you focus your conscious attention upon is being reinforced as if it were actually happening, thousands of times per second.

If you want someone to feel well, avoid discussing his sickness or his emotional wounds. If you want someone to perform more efficiently, avoid belaboring her mistakes. If you want someone to feel comfortable around you, use her labels for things instead of yours. Remember, you are a "someone" too, and this applies to the words you use in your head. Some people employ a horribly corrosive internal vocabulary and strident mental tones of voice while steering the course of their lives. Computer people have a saying, "Garbage In, Garbage Out". If you use nasty language in your head, you will find yourself dredging up all the nasty experiential references associated with the words you use—just to make sense of them. Don't be surprised if you produce more of the very things you *don't* want—emotionally, mentally and behaviorally.

Finally, avoid pushing yourself to verbally recall or initiate events. You know that when you try to remember the name of an actress or a song, the more you consciously dig for the association, the harder it is to recall the name. Your conscious effort draws the name tantalizingly close—just outside consciousness. If you put your conscious attention on something else entirely instead of trying to dictate recollection or creativity, that particular experience is much more likely to pop into your head two seconds *after* you start thinking about something else.

Appreciating the option of turning your attention away from your desired outcome brings up the fifth, and possibly most valuable, fact about the different "oceans" in everyone's head— Transderivational Processing leaves things out. Salvador Dali once said, "It's a wonder that, of all the things that *could* happen, how few ever actually do."

While you concentrated on an "ocean," what happened to all the cows? Or politicians? Or that thing that was right on the tip of your tongue? Not only did you reinforce the stored experiences associated with the words you focused on, but you dropped everything else a little further back from the "front" of your mind momentarily. If your Train ran backwards, with the words first, that would be great.

Because those aspects of human life which are hardest to put into words are likely to be those portions of life we wrestle with the hardest, it's helpful to remember this last aspect of what your mind does in response to words. Words are easy, and they are seductive.

When all those oceans rush to compete for your conscious attention, you are likely to forget that real life rarely if ever lends itself to simple, verbal solutions. All those oceans flowing into your Caboose might mask the fact that everything else has just receded a bit further from the shores of consciousness. You might fail to notice that your Train is back on autopilot again. Be reinforcing the use of single-word solutions and goals for action, like single-issue interest groups or individuals fixed on their one active Ingredient for happiness, we can actively impoverish our lives. By pushing other experiences further and further out of sight, repeating our magic words again and again, the Train travels the same old tracks, in the same old way, and we end up bitterly wishing the same old stuff wouldn't keep happening. Then, if we're not very careful, we'll go shopping for a new "ocean," instead of new experiences in the company of other primates.

o   o   o

Labels aren't real. People and their behaviors are.

3

Avoiding the Hypothetical Life

I wrote about The Train of Thought at some length in the previous chapters. But now I want to make absolutely clear how words occur *after the fact of a thought,* making them the Caboose on The Train of Thought. The importance of this concept becomes clear when you know how the mind processes words and language.

To get started, grab a piece of paper and a pen. Now, sort through your memory for the first time you experienced what it is like to love someone. The person can be a child, a parent or a partner from the present or the past.

While that moment comes into your mind, search for something humorous that happened to you. Think of a recent time when you burst into laughter at something which struck you as really funny.

Finally, quickly recall a moment when you felt truly sorry for somebody. The emotion accompanying the image can be compassion, pity or just sadness. When all three experiences are in place, begin to examine the last one.

Now, while you revive the memory in as lively detail as possible, imagine that moment is temporarily interrupted by someone tapping you on the shoulder and asking, "Why are you so sad?" Jot down what you would have said.

Now go to experience number two, the funny one. Imagine, as you bring the moment to the front of your mind as vividly as possible so that the corners of your mouth even start to turn up with laughter, that someone pops up again, taps you on the shoulder and demands to know, "What's so funny?" Jot down your answer.

Do the same thing with the experience of loving, with one little shift. When you go back in your mind to experience the emotion of love, imagine at the same moment that the person who is the object of your love is approaching you and asks, "Why do you love me?" Note that answer as well.

Take a look at all three answers and consider the following: If you review all three experiences in their original forms again, clearly and distinctly, can you find any of those phrases in the *original* experiences which you later wrote down to describe them?

When you felt sorry for that person, did the feeling and all its accompanying emotional reactions precede or follow whatever you said to yourself at the time? When you burst out laughing, did you first stop to explain the humor to yourself, or did you just laugh?

Have you ever been able to adequately put into words that moment when your feeling of love for someone fills your heart to the brim.

In reviewing the situations, you may have noticed that the mental process associated with each moment may have been accompanied by images, even sounds or words. Are you now aware that when it comes to love, laughter and sorrow, the verbal explanation of the reaction is usually tacked-on after you've begun reacting and not before?

You may have discovered that the verbal descriptions you wrote down contained some of the same words as the original conversation. But again, those words did not emerge until you *asked* for them.

At first this may seem like common sense, or even unimportant to some people. But when we understand that our mind provides us with sensations and habits for acting and thinking, and then furnishes the words to describe them after the fact so that we can talk about them, it can revolutionize the way we act.

How many times have you had a five-point plan presented to you on how to react in the future differently than you have in the past? How often has someone asked for a description of the words you said in your head which caused you to act loving, or to laugh, or be sad, or depressed, or unconcerned ? How often did you get the distinct impression that words were inadequate to describe an experience?

The media presents us with verbal explanations about other people's experiences as if those words were the source itself. Newscasters tell us about the discussions in Congress which create and pass legislation. TV psychologists tell us the five things that have gone through a mass murderer's head each the time he killed. Soap opera stars tell us the words they say in their heads which lead them directly to their next melodramatic problem . Shows for children inform their audience of kids the seven questions they must ask themselves to discover if feeling badly about "strange men" is appropriate.

The fact is we do not engage in an internal dialogue prior to each emotional, mental or behavioral response. We simply respond, and if we pay attention, we can elaborate by using a description of that response—during or after the fact.

You may be surprised to discover this, but the vast majority of your mind's functions or "thinking" takes place without any dialogue at all in or out of consciousness. As creatures of habit, we usually are on automatic pilot at the important moments. Whereas dialogue and step-by-step verbal thinking are solely a conscious act.

In order to make this simple to grasp, do the following:

Talk yourself into an orgasm. Now, talk yourself out of a belief. If you are a Democrat, please convince yourself to become a Republican. Talk yourself out of liking your favorite food. Talk yourself into falling in love. Tell yourself a funny story. When you attempt any of these things, you can clearly demonstrate that the words you used to describe or question the experiences in your head came last in the thinking process.

Words are truly the caboose of human relations.

When humans began walking erect they didn't have the sophisticated linguistic skills we have today. Symbolic language structures are a recent accomplishment and are dwarfed by the thousands of years when humans conversed in grunts and signals.

Long before we were able to hold an intelligent conversation on what's right and what's wrong, we already had built the foundation for patterns of acting in certain ways. We developed the habit of expecting specific feelings and behaviors, and we came to the conclusion, after the fact, that we held certain beliefs about what makes up "right and wrong."

In other words, we didn't all read a book and exclaim, "Yep, what's mine is mine and what's yours is mine if I can get it." First came the actions, their rehearsal and reinforcement, then came the vocabulary with its value judgements, beliefs and moral distinctions.

So, how can the current trend in our culture to put words first be harmful to the consumer's mind?

One answer is that we become seduced into substituting the caboose of words for the whole train of thought and action when we find ourselves in trouble. The illusion is fostered that we can master any part of our life if only we can just adequately describe it. We are frequently invited to act as if saying something is as good as doing it. This helps us pretend that we have much more direct control over the world and our minds than we actually do.

The illusion of conscious control over anything sells well, even if it doesn't work well. How often have you heard advertising for a program which will help you control your life? It can come at you during newscast commentaries, infomercials, psychological analysis TV-style, or from out of the mouth of your boss or your spouse. Perhaps these phrases sound familiar:

"Take charge of your life today!"

"The answer is actually quite simple!"

"It's obvious why you've failed so far!"

"And do you know why?"

"Stop taking everything so seriously!"

"Tell me what you were thinking at the time."

"All you have to do is understand..."

"Use the power of your mind, now!"

Implicit in each of these phrases and hundreds more we use in conversation every day, is an advertisement for putting the caboose before the train. We've segmented our world into several smaller worlds according to the vocabularies we bring to bear to try to control life within each segment. How many of us have gotten into the habit of thinking we are a different person at work than we are at home? What's actually different? Our clothes, our vocabulary, the people we see, some things we do.

But is our brain, or our body and mind, different at work than at home? We do not put on new personalities—new habits of thought and action with our wingtips and Daytimers. By creating and reinforcing these artificial boundaries from place-to-place in our lives, we also reinforce the illusion of control. Then we sell and purchase more "control words" when last years' models fail.

Wherever we are, whatever the activity may be, we pick up thousands of unintended, implicit suggestions that invite a discussion in our minds before we act. We become more likely to buy an improvement scheme that claims easy solutions to problems if we learn just the right words to say to ourselves. What's more, there are actually several industries devoted to the sale, care and feeding of the words-first approach, and they advertise the back-to-front approach directly.

We have created and support a huge personal growth industry which has over 200 different words for sale in the guise of diseases, disorders and dysfunctions. Some people attempt to buy the answers to all problems in life as if they represented a single, well-defined curable illness. Having settled their attention on what they'll tell themselves about the future, they presume salvation rests at the end of an easily explained, easily understood track of the seven steps to cure disease, or to correct personal impediments to success.

In the personal development business there are a vast number of classes, seminars, books and tapes along with continuing education programs, and self-discovery retreats of an unimaginable variety. Each one suggests that we give some serious thought to "Why we are not happy," or "Why we need to adopt *this* simple, easy solution," or "How to take these seven written steps to personal fulfillment"—batteries not included.

We have built an even larger professional development

industry which sells business people simple solutions like *"Powerful Marketing Techniques," "The Power of Excellent Rapport," "Empowerment for Employees"* and *"One Million and Seven Powerful Closing Techniques,"* all written typically with a script of internal dialogue to explain each step of human interaction before we are required to try to live it.

But probably the most limiting aspect of improvement schemes which put words before action is the tendency to recommend specific, verbally-defined goals for people. Human beings are notoriously non-specific and ill-defined in their daily living. They also are likely to ask for more of what they've gotten in the past, simply out of habit. And they have gotten the notion over and over that setting very specific, verbal goals is the way to accomplish things in this world—both at work and at home.

You know that isn't so and you can prove it.

Can you recall the last time you outlined a specific goal which required the participation of other people and which came to fruition precisely the way you planned it? Did everything happen as planned in your marriage, for example, or in the raising of your children? How about your job, or the events in your senior year? What about your last relationship, or life with that beautiful car?

Outlines, profiles, surveys and multi-step plans are not brain-friendly. They require you to attempt to reverse the natural order in which your brain works. Organizational charts, quantitative evaluations of performance and quarterly deportment goals are not brain-friendly. Neither are diagnostic labels used to attempt to promote mental or physical health.

Even a goal like personal happiness, held constantly in your consciousness, verbally repeated and reinforced, is not brain-friendly. It requires you to place your attention at the rear of the train—on the words. Of course, you will have many more associations for "happiness" near the front of your mind, but they won't stay the same and other valuable experiences recede from consciousness at the same time. Most folks need other people to contribute to their lives in order to be happy.

You can't steer from the rear of the train: you can only ride. And if the train isn't steered actively in a new direction, your habit-producing mind will simply follow the track it has followed before. The more attention you spend in your head talking about how you wish the world would bend to your control, the less attention you will have left to respond to what the world and the people in it are actually providing for you.

Success, happiness, fulfillment, quality, satisfaction and all the other well-worn words with which we are daily tempted to wish upon in our heads are just linguistic distractions. If we buy the illusion of control, we will inevitably have little attention left to notice our conduct among other people in the world. It is our daily contact with others which determines our successes or failures.

The wise person recognizes that human interactions are not scripted. They are rarely accomplished with a definable beginning, a clear middle and a predictable ending. Think of the last relationship you had with another person. When it ended, was that really *the* end? Or did some of it linger? You know people who, upon getting divorced, ran right out and married someone just like the partner they shed. You know others who find someone like their parents, and still others who weave the thread of old relationships into every new conversation.

The patterns of thinking during our work days are no different from our personal ones—although the distractions of paper, policies and procedures tend to reinforce words-before-reality even more strongly there. W. Edward Deming, the father of Total Quality, insists that numerical goals, ranking and rating workers, merit systems and other quantitative verbal structures "destroy morale and diminish quality." He calls them the forces of destruction. They pass over the human factor in favor of words.

The less attention you pay to paper and the more attention you give to people, the more self-reliant you will act. If you must deal with paper, profiles and pronouncements, use them as general directions, not as destinations.

Avoid the trap of the hypothetical life. Keep yourself away from the person so obsessed with the numbers and predictions that he can't "have a nice day" unless his numbers tell him to— especially the numbers on a scale. Numbers and outlines are not brain-friendly. If you doubt it, ask the parent how effective that ten-minute stretch of "quality time" with her six-year-old that would shape his life, between 4:47 and 4:57 pm, turned out to be.

There are a great many popular programs on "creative problem-solving" and "managing creativity." When you next hear a seductive phrase such as "managing creativity" beckoning you to your caboose, place it back in the real world context of human interactions and see the fancy words for what they are: "managed creativity" is like "planned spontaneity."

When you catch yourself discussing a situation at a time when you could be living it, stop and take a deep breath, and as you exhale find out how pleasant it is to push yourself up from the chair, out of your head, and toward the engine.

If you appreciate the fact that we all function today much the way we did before we learned our symbolic language, both as individuals and as a species, you could be in luck. You might remember to pay attention to the life you are living, rather than the one you are describing. Remember the "love, laughter and sorrow" exercise and know that descriptions of life's most valuable moments are always inadequate .

Certainly, if you make a conscious effort to shift the dialogue you use in your head from critical phrases and tones toward more constructive statements, that is an improvement. It is helpful also to recall that once you've changed what you say to yourself, you still haven't produced anything which will help sustain and build on those nice noises in your head. Please talk nicely when you talk in your head, and please stay out of your head as much as possible so you can *act* well, too.

What applies to you and your mind goes double for other people. If you wish to begin practicing a more brain-friendly "words-last" approach, remember to include the people around you. Interrupt yourself when you catch yourself attending to only half of what somebody does and says. Stop finishing people's sentences, telling yourself that you know what they *really* mean. To paraphrase the pro-gun lobby, "Words don't help people, *people* help people!"

Save that discussion for when you are alone, and pull your conscious attention out of your head. That way you can focus on all the things you've missed while you were busy talking to yourself. "Sorry, could you say that again, please?" Sound familiar?

Other people cannot hear your inner voice, so they are much more likely to judge and respond to you based on your performance. Somewhere along the line, someone else may hold the key to that door you've been wishfully talking to yourself about all your life. I hope your attention's out of your caboose at that moment, so you can notice and receive it.

o   o   o

Interpretation of experiences is a poor substitute for new experiences. Concentrating on rational can only reinforce old habits, not develop new ones.

4

But ... Why?

eing creatures of habit makes people uncomfortable on occasion. When somebody catches you acting in a way you told yourself—and probably them as well—that you'd never do again, you feel uncomfortable. When you do something the same old way having just succeeded last week doing it a new way, you feel uncomfortable. When you call somebody on the phone and as it rings realize you have forgotten who you were calling, you feel uncomfortable. And, most frequently, when you do something without thinking about it at the time and somebody calls you on it later, boy, do ever you feel uncomfortable.

To demonstrate this point, try the following exercise:

Sit down and list three things you did recently which succeeded. Then list three things you did which you wish you could do over again differently. Now go back over each item and write down the reason why you did each one.

Now go back over each item and write down the reasons your boss or a coworker would give as your reasons. That is, create a set of different reasons they might give for your actions. And make sure they are plausible.

Now go back over each item and write down the different reasons a total stranger, looking in on your life, might give for you the way you did these things different from the previous ones.

Finally, write other reasons for each item that your mother might give, a psychologist might give, a policewoman, your minister and your third grade teacher. All reasons must be plausible, and different.

If you get stuck for ideas, simply turn on your radio or TV and find either a call-in talk show, or a round-table newscast with several different experts. Listen for ten minutes and you'll have more *"why-I-did-its"* than you can shake a stick at. Pick from among those you consider plausible, although you will be applying them to completely different events.

Ask yourself just one question: Which reasons are the right ones?

What if I were to tell you that reasons you have chosen are wrong? How long would it take you to come up with a really fine idea to prove that you were right? And if I were somehow able to show you—in front of other people—that your reasons for proving me wrong were absurd, how long would it take you to find a *brand new* set of reasons why you were right and I was *still* wrong? Fun, isn't it?

You have just demonstrated that in a matter of minutes you can generate different lists of reasons for the very same action, and they are all plausible. Yet many people insist that there is only one way to think about something, one reason for an action. These people are mistaken.

Whenever you place your conscious attention on something

you just said, did, or felt and ask, "Why?" a small part of your mind generates a whole bunch of answers. They all line up on top of one another like candy in a *Pez* dispenser. Then, if the first "Well, because I..." doesn't work, your mind knocks the top one off the stack, and the rest move up one notch. Your mouth then opens, and out pops another response like : "What I *really* meant was I..." If that excuse doesn't work, there are plenty more where it came from.

These typical responses should again demonstrate why the mind doesn't start with reasons for actions. Actions result from habitual responses the mind has learned. We are basically habit-building organisms, and thank God for that. How would you like to be forced to relearn how to get through a rectangular hole in the wall every single time you approached a door?

Most people are trained from an early age to believe that the mind works on reasons, rather than habits. Every moment of the day, we are bombarded with direct and indirect advertising which suggests that we must control our minds in ways which are doomed to fail—a fact which leaves us frustrated. As most current brain research confirms, reasons for actions usually *follow* the event.

We are influenced to use what I call *Active Ingredients* by habit. Active Ingredients are the "easy explanations" for habits of thinking blended with action that keep over 90 percent of our mind working at any given moment. We've practiced this simple, easy solution routine for a long time. Yet despite the fact that nine out of ten times any act you perform is done *without* thinking about it, you are still encouraged to ask "Why?"

Advertising *Active Ingredients* (or the answer to the "why" in human reactions) as a market commodity began in America mainly through the efforts of two men: Napoleon Hill and Norman Vincent Peale. Hill worked in the business community and Peale addressed his message to the personal development industry.

These two experts called their active ingredients "Positive Mental Attitude" and just plain "Positive Attitude," respectively.

Eager to have their questions apparently answered and their problems seemingly solved, Americans grabbed the phrases these men advertised and have continued to for years. Thousands of other "why merchants" have since followed suit with their own active ingredients, but it was "Positive Attitude" which was the first, best-selling *Active Ingredient* in America.

Whether you buy Power, Control, Responsibility, Codependency, Total Quality, Introverted-drive, Motivation, Self-esteem or Accountability as *the* reason for why you will succeed or fail forever this week, you have bought a ghost. These noises are not things. They only have meaning for you. No one else reacts to them exactly the way you do. Worse, in order to pay attention to them, you are required to spend more time in the caboose of your train of thought talking about them in your head. The use of verbal *Active Ingredients* to explain your actions, guide your mind, or improve your life requires that you ignore the world of human interaction and escape into your head.

The good news is that in your head you can *always* make these Active Ingredients accurate, true and effective. The bad news is that nobody else lives in your head.

For an object lesson, grab a chair and stand next to it for a moment. Now, look toward the entrance to the room and imagine a hungry, growling Bengal tiger approaching with its fangs bared and glistening, eyes fixed on your throat, powerful claws ready to cut you to shreds. The cat is ready to pounce. To defend yourself you have one second to make the choice between picking up the chair or hitting the tiger right on the snout with a great

big motivation. Of course, the idea of searching for a motivation when you are in danger is absurd. The habit of survival is so ingrained that the only action possible is grabbing the chair. But the exercise demonstrates how putting theory before practice is not something we do naturally: it is learned behavior.
Our habit-forming patterns start at an early age. I remember when I was about six, I had grabbed a forest green crayon, got down on my knees and was going to do some serious coloring on a piece of paper spread on the glossy parquet floor. You could tell I was serious, because instead of holding the crayon like a pencil, I clutched it in a vise-like grip with my fist.

As a child, I had very little trouble getting "lost in thought," (adults often do, too). I was soon lost in coloring and unaware I moved past the edges of my coloring paper all the way to the closet wall. It was only when I stopped, stepped back and looked at the newly-decorated wall that reality rushed in on me. I was not dumb: I fled to my room.

When my mother called me into the den in that tone of voice she saved for such occasions, the advertising and learning began. I was scared as any kid in trouble. She asked me, over and over again, in no uncertain tones, "Why?" She acted as if my furnishing her with a reason for doing something silly would let her feel better about it.

I had learned from repeated experiences not to tell the truth. I had learned early that "I don't know" is not an adequate answer.

I wasn't thinking about *why* I should color the wall before I did it. I had no reason. I wasn't thinking (consciously) about reasons. I did what we all learn to do in these circumstances—I made something up.

There was mother yelling, "Give me one good reason why you did that!" There I was, in trouble and learning fast that I had to have a reason. Presto! I learned that when we are in trouble, reasons are good! I threw the first active ingredient that popped into my mind at her. It may actually have been a thought which could have been flitting through my mind at the time of the crime, but it certainly wasn't the reason—the one and only reason— which I gave myself *before* I started coloring. There *was no reason!* If she sighed and rolled her eyes, even before I started speaking, I had learned to switch the reason I was making up in mid-sentence—and start in with a different one. I would do that until I ran out of ideas, and as a last ditch effort, I cried.

Think of the last time you built a list of excuses to explain your behavior at work. You heard one of your superiors was displeased with your performance on a project. You immediately started to rattle off reasons to explain the problem away while your *Pez* dispenser was popping up new ones at a steady rate.

The thing about spring-loaded, multiple explanations is that they are all true, and they are all false. One reason after another pops with ease from the mind's spring-propelled recesses. What they all have in common is that they are unthinkingly generated by our mind anytime a habitual feeling or action appears in our consciousness—just in case somebody asks us why we did that.

We have given so little reinforcement to approaches which emphasize experiences over reasons that it is no wonder that the *Active Ingredient* has taken the lion's share of the consumer mind market. For years we have invested in efforts to divide our lives up into various compartments—work, home, personal, romance, parenthood, and so on. Then we have labeled the "forces" which explain our responses in each compartment (motivation, quality time, self-esteem, mutual understanding, unconditional love) as if they were as definable and solid as a chair.

If you find this hard to swallow, just try to pour yourself a cup of happiness.

Like my mother, we have gotten into the habit of feeling more comfortable if we have a reason—any reason—for our actions. To protect yourself and the people you live with from buying any more of that kind of advertising, it would be helpful to remember that not only is there no self-talk prior to each reaction you have, but there is also no single reason motivating you to react that way. To be totally accurate, there are plenty of reasons—dozens perhaps—but they are all generated after the fact of the reaction and are just as true in regards to your response as they are false.

The important thing for the informed consumer to practice recognizing is that, no matter how plausible they may sound, reasons do not provoke your mind to act; they are generated to excuse your mind's actions.

So, what *do* you do when someone asks you, "Why did you do that?" Tell her the truth. Say, "I'm not really sure. Why do *you* think I did?" She'll tell you what she's already been saying about you in the Caboose of her train of thought, and you'll have a chance to respond appropriately.

While you manufacture reasons why things are wrong, reasons to fix them, and reasons for doing it "just this way", time is ticking by. Time is one thing we do not have an unlimited supply of. When it runs out for each of us, it's gone. And with it go all our options for new or different experiences. By trying to understand the "why" of our lives, we frequently miss any new "whats" in it. Relying on the conscious, verbal Caboose of words wastes time and keeps us that much more focused on what we *don't* want. It is counter-productive.

For the better part of this century, we've gotten used to buying reasons, or *doubly* limiting ourselves by finding reasons to eliminate and replace other reasons which didn't adequately explain anything in the first place! So that, today, we find ourselves awash in the unfortunate habit of not only demanding explanations for things we think and do out of habit, but also insisting those solutions all be "new and improved".

We have forgotten that sitting in a circle with managers intent upon defining, reviewing and revising lists of "the best" seven quality performance goals for employees just might hurt more than it helps. We have forgotten that talking about why we have problems may be the kind of "support" we don't need. We have forgotten there is a difference between theory and practice.

Have you ever attended a support group, a quality circle or a focus group with the goal to raise Self-Esteem? This is like treating a motivation as if it were as real as a chair. Instead, try picking a group like Big Brothers or Big Sisters, The Red Cross, Project Literacy, Habitat for Humanity or a church volunteer group if you want to seek esteem in a group setting. Self-esteem is the conscious afterthought of *acting* in ways which are worthy of regard.

If you want to practice protecting yourself against our culture's habit of focusing attention on the reasons for acting prior to really acting more beneficially, here are a couple of easy exercises which you will have fun doing.

Listen to those TV and radio shows where the active ingredients for everything from bisexuality to the falling dollar fly fast and furious every day. Then do the exercise you started with:come up with at least three more equally plausible reasons why the person who's talking is right, but they have to be reasons different from the ones the person used. Since you have a built-in Pez dispenser, you may as well use it *consciously* to remind yourself daily that one reason is as good (and made-up) as another. You'll find yourself acting less distressed about somebody else's "right" reasons, real soon.

If you have someone else you see regularly who has read

this book, you can do the exercise I gave to a group of teachers. They all did a few demonstrations to prove to themselves that one "why" was just as true, and false, as another "why," whether it was "confidence," "self-control" or the dreaded "attention-deficit hyperactivity disorder." In their staff meetings and consulting sessions thereafter, when someone inevitably slipped back into the habit of actually believing his reason was the one and only right reason, all the others agreed to pantomime repeatedly flipping open the tops of imaginary Pez dispensers while whispering, "Pez, Pez, Pez..." until the forgetful one caught on and laughed.

Finally, when you find yourself tempted to resort to rumination in your Caboose about why you haven't yet improved some portion of your reactions to life, take a deep breath, push yourself out of your chair and notice how much more comfortable you feel sighing and substituting something like, "I wonder how soon I'll find something more valuable to *do.*" Then go find it.

o   o   o

Reasons we give for actions are convenient to the moment, but "Active Ingredients" do not deliver the results they promise.

"*Speech is conveniently located between thought and action where it often substitutes for both.*"

John Andrew Holmes

5

Me, Myself and I

Because words come last, not first, in your mind's actions, it would be wise to avoid responding to any advertising, overt or more subtle, which encourages you to improve by starting with words. But there is such a deeply ingrained habit in our culture which points you away from interactions and into your Caboose to begin building an alternative habit for directing your mind.

Grab a piece of paper and give the following exercise some attention.

Pretend you are a manager of a business (even if you are one). Think for a minute about the type of people you want working for you. Now write down what you consider to be the top five qualities essential for a person to have if he is going to be a good employee in your business.

Set that list aside, and consider what the top five qualities are that a good parent cannot do without. Write those down, too.

Now, start one final list. On this one, give some serious thought to what five qualities you need to accomplish what you would like to in your personal relationships from this point forward.

Now pull all three lists together. You have fifteen qualities. Or do you? From my experience, I'll bet you have fifteen great beginnings which have less practical application than you think. The words you've put down have some deep and present meaning for you. It is likely that if you were to use these words in a meeting of managers, or the PTA, or with your favorite person, that some people would nod their heads with encouragement when they heard the words leave your lips. After all, they are obviously labels for some pretty important experiences stored somewhere in your head. It's the "in your head" part that you would be wise to consider carefully if you want the words to remain brain-friendly when you try to put them to work *outside* your head.

This story may give you some insight into the dangers of expecting everybody else to live inside *your* Caboose.

A colleague of mine, Paul, was called into a large manufacturing company on the east coast for consulting work. While he was with the organization an interesting thing happened.

A hugely successful best-selling business book about "Excellence" was published. Everybody in the organization had read this book, including, it appeared, the CEO of this company. Paul sat in on a big meeting of all the regional directors of the company, and the CEO marched to the podium with the book in his hand and read long sections of the book to the assembled people in the room. All these people got a chance to sit back and listen to stories about how others had demonstrated "excellence" in their business. All the stories had happy endings. All the people got lost in thoughts of excellence.

Then the CEO slammed the book shut, stepped back and said, "And I want this implemented within the quarter, or heads will roll!" He stormed out of the room.

Can you guess what happened next? Those of you who have been in this type of meeting will know that a nervous silence ensued. That was followed by some shifting, some hemming and hawing. Finally, one director turned to another and said, "Well, I don't see much trouble with marketing, but I'm a little concerned about implementing excellence in finance. What do you think, Harry?"

None of the people in the meeting had a clue how to put "excellence" into their portion of the organization. The only comfort all of them could take was from discovering that everybody was apparently equally without inspiration, although no one would come right out and say so.

Think of it. The CEO had some wonderful experiences which were sharpened in his mind by association to the words in the book. The directors had some nice experiences of their own associated with those words. But when they were forced to consider actually implementing some of the ideas in the book with the real people they worked with, they all got a big dose of the difference between theory and practice.

Way back in my early work in human service, I worked in a chemical dependency treatment facility. I ran afoul of the same discrepancy between verbal mind-movies which are encouraged by evocative labels, and the attempt to get people in the real world to implement the experiences behind the labels.

I had a young man in my group who had been arrested for beating another man's head against a wall during a fight he had picked in a bar. This was his third assault conviction, and his choice was between alcoholism treatment or spending up to 14 years in the penitentiary. He was built like an iron wedge, with long black hair, and a lot of black leather clothing.

In his intake, I discovered that this young man's father had spent the boy's entire youth getting drunk, getting angry and then beating anything that moved in front of him—usually the boy's mother. Once, when he was five, the boy got between them accidentally, and the father broke a chair over the boy's back.

Guess what everybody in the boy's experience called the father...in mixed company? An *alcoholic*.

Stop for a moment and recall how the mind actually works. That word was associated with lots and lots of less-than-comfortable experiences in that child's head. As a matter of fact, anytime that word was mentioned around the boy, all those experiences rushed right back to the front of his mind where they reinforced themselves.

But my head held totally different associations for that word. As the professional in the field, with my limited knowledge of the mind's actual functions at the time, I thought that word was magic. I must have, judging from what I expected to happen from using it in my group.

You see, I was trained at the time when a patient was "in denial" and not "recovering" if he failed to apply the term "alcoholic" to himself. I had come to believe that the people in my group were beyond my help unless they first started by proclaiming themselves to be alcoholics. The rest of their life experiences meant nothing compared to the importance of describing themselves with that word.

Naturally, if I had pulled my head out of my own Caboose momentarily, I might have recognized that the young man I was counseling may not have shared many of my own preconceptions about the distinction of the word "alcoholic." But I didn't.

The day came for me to push him to admit out loud exactly what he was, so he could start getting better. I began like I usually did, saying, "Okay. If you admit you're an alcoholic, you're an alcoholic. If you deny you're an alcoholic, since denial is a primary aspect of the disease, then you're an alcoholic, anyway."

To give the moment some punch, I relied upon peer pressure to help him make the admission I sought. I said, "You know that alcoholism, whether you admit it or not, is a chronic, progressive and terminal illness, one-hundred percent fatal if left unchecked. All these other nice men in this group whom you've just started to care for didn't get here by mistake. They are all *dying* to hear what you have to say. So...stop stalling and tell us what you are! If you admit you're an alcoholic, you are one. And if you deny you are one, you are one anyway! So, everybody's dying to hear—what are you?"

If you have any lingering confusion about the mind working first out of habit, what happened to me next will probably clear it right up.

He picked up his chair—just like his father the *alcoholic* had years before—and began advancing toward me through the circle of chairs. Under their breaths, all the men in the room whom I had "shared" similar "help" with, were expressing their gratitude towards me by urging him on: "Do it!"

He stood over me, metal chair raised over his head, while he (and I) sweated. I sent the rest of the group out of the room. When he finally threw the chair, over my head, it hit the wall so hard that it stuck in the wallboard. He broke, smashed and ruined furniture, leaving a wake of destruction behind as he threw his things together and left the treatment center. I signed him out officially as leaving against medical advice. That meant that when he surfaced, he would be escorted directly to Stillwater State Pen to begin serving up to 14 years in prison.

Prison. All because he refused to identify his entire being, his whole self, with one lousy word. To me, it was a magic word. To him, obviously, it wasn't.

To the CEO—and to his subordinates—"excellence" was a magic word. But to the folks who had to implement whatever "excellence" meant to the CEO, its magic wore thin real fast.

The bottom-line danger of our culture's attempts to put words before experience in human relations is that it requires you to act and think that what's going on inside your head is somehow more important than anyone else's.

You become convinced of this by being encouraged to focus your attention on the Caboose of words in your own head, and learning to act as if you hold the true secret to what is right, worthwhile, healthy—not only for yourself, but for everyone else.

When a journey of a lifetime dead-ends at a specific, consciously-defined destination, major difficulties arise. The person doing the imagining discovers to his deep disappointment that his heart's desire and his worst nightmare both actually reside somewhere "outside" of himself, usually just out of reach. Remember, whatever success and failure are to you, their accomplishment still relies on the direct and indirect contributions of other people. When someone defines his goal for the rest of his life as "happiness," a part of his mind immediately discovers that "happy" has a lot in common with "motivation." It seems as solid as a chair until you reach to pick it up. The double-bind your mind faces when defining your aims and pitfalls as labels is that these ideas become abstractions like "excellence."

Worse, though you seem to have created this ideal in your mind, you have much less control over it than you have been led to believe. All of us learn that happiness is an outside agent which we believe we deserve, but don't yet have. And you are encouraged to act as if you have control over your ideal. You take the attitude that it is your destination or nothing. It's a short step from there to "It's my destination or else."

This is not a new development. It was Descartes who said, "I think, therefore I am." After advertising and twisting that notion for a couple of centuries we've arrived at a place on our cultural journey where all these well-advertised, but insubstantial active ingredients are merely steps to a personal goal or impediments to it. The goal becomes paramount and the uninformed consumer practices habits of thinking and acting which may devalue other people as if they were nothing but labels in the Caboose: "*My* focus group, *my* support group, my relationship, my hostile boss, my difficult colleague, my buyers, my company."

Descartes himself disavowed the effort to put his "inside versus outside" approach to work to understand human beings. He warned that the Scientific Method, or the single simple solution approach, would never work on human beings. Ongoing experience would not hold still to be measured, defined and understood, he warned, but we failed to listen.

We Americans enjoy the right to pursue happiness among our many freedoms. But the presumption of control required for a solely self-determined destination may mean the change of the meaning of happiness from an outgrowth of something I do among others called *pursuing* into something I can acquire for—and by—myself. Pursuing is discarded in favor of just "having." It soon becomes not a want, but a need, something you not only can have, but *should* have. Instead of having a right to pursue it, a person may act as if he has the unchallenged right to deserve it by virtue of nothing but his own desire. Happiness is solidified into a destination in his head: a product in the marketplace he must, should and will own.

People who indulge this illusion of control over their pursuits build a presumption of entitlement. This presumption is shot throughout our culture and is not exclusive to those recipients of programs going by that label. We are inundated daily by both intentional and implicit advertising which sells the notion that everyone should have the chance to get everything exactly the way she specifies her own everything should be. The fact that it is physically impossible to translate a mental movie into identical experiences for all people is missed entirely.

But, following this approach, vast numbers of Americans become victims or blamers. While holding their disease or injustice constantly defined in their mind, thousands of victims ask doctors, lawyers and social workers to get them compensation for that happiness they were deprived of by a poor upbringing, sexual infidelity, sexual discrimination, cultural bias, body dismorphic disorder (people who think they're ugly), diminished capacity, "uncontrolled impulse syndrome," or obnoxious personality disorder. The blamers hire the same lawyers, social workers, legislators and lobbyists to stop others from doing what they do. This ultimate reduction of a life's pursuit to the demand for one active ingredient makes a shambles of family and community and creates a nation filled with single-issue zealots.

What few of these people notice is that they sow more discontent than the content they reap. As Descartes warned, when you try to master your universe by insisting that all human experience fits inside the false advertising of "objective realities"— like Happiness, Control, Motivation, Justice, Independence, Responsibility—you lose more than you gain. Putting words before people and experience is not brain-friendly activity. People and experiences *outside* your Caboose determine your successes and failures in life, resulting in more brain-friendly ways of relating to other people.

If the time you spend with others is going to be directed towards goals and objectives, make it your business to find out what labels each of those people uses to represent those goals to him or herself. Then, when you are with them, just as if you were visiting a foreign country with a different language, use their words for the goals and not yours.

Avoid the self-aggrandizing habit of reducing another person's activities, emotional life or past performances into some catchy verbal formula. It hurts both of you to take one experience, or a set of similar ones, and define the whole person in your head as your label for those experiences. Any phrase that begins, "Well, that's just because she's a ..." or "Didn't you know he has ..." would be a good place to start substituting actions for words. Brian Tracy, the famous sales trainer, says that profiles which label people may be true for psychology, but have no place in business. They have no place in psychology, either.

Avoid the temptation to argue for your limitations. Although this trick is advertised liberally, it is rarely helpful. The world is filled with active ingredients, formal and informal, sold to help excuse your lack of achievement. But, whether you selected "shyness" or "post-traumatic stress disorder," whether you bought "addictive personality disorder," "resistance" or "lack of motivation," whether people tell you you're suffering from "stress," "pressure," "family dysfunction," "organizational impairment," "immaturity" or whatever, this method of concentrating on what you *don't* want is likely to lead you astray.

No matter how much you wish to, you're never really going to understand what someone else meant. Practice in juggling—rather than swallowing—words and labels will help you overcome the temptation to try. That could leave lots more time and attention to follow their lead instead of your labels.

When it comes to guiding your actions among people at

work and at play, use no systems with more than three steps, no approaches which require you to learn a new vocabulary to accomplish something, no rules for conduct which substitute outlines for people, no methods which require you to survey yourself and others to find your compatabilities and selling points— in short, no program for perfection which asks you to substitute paper, policies or procedures for people. (Inventory the time, money and energy you spend each day on paper-generated, or related, activities versus people-generated, or related, activities, and you will discover the size of this task.)

Remember your list of qualities. When you hear someone else's, imagine that he is just as drawn to his magic words as you were toward yours. Remember that words do tend to reinforce the experiences associated with them in the mind of the beholder. Avoid correcting their words, and avoid taking yours too seriously. Remember especially that innovation and different reactions can be diminished in your repertoire by concentrating on evocative, but empty labels.

On the other hand, because your mind will reinforce the experiences you have referenced to the words you use, start interrupting yourself—out loud or in your head—when you catch yourself indulging in any words-first attempts to control your mind especially if they are critical words. Common sense dictates that you use more productive language than corrosive and critical dialogue with yourself and others. But avoid the temptation to take the nice sensation that accompanies nice self-talk as the indication that you've actually accomplished anything more than getting ready to act in more valuable ways.

Last, watch out for the No-Pain, No-Gain myth. Because we've spent several hundred years reinforcing the figure-things-out-first approaches, most of us have adopted the habit of looking for reasons at the exact moment when it would be most harmful to do so. When you are in pain, emotionally or mentally, you would be well-advised to act as if you were in physical pain. You don't meditate on your upbringing to find the cause of your broken arm before getting it set. The same applies when you do, or say, something which causes you or others pain. Act first, and talk about it later. That's the way the mind works best. Lean in the direction you want to fall; keep your head out of the Caboose, and into your daily life as much as possible.

The good news is that if you act as if labels follow experiences, you will find you don't have to share the responsibility for your successes among others in the real world with active ingredients and outside agents in your head. You get all the credit for what you do.

The bad news is, you also get all the credit for what you do. If you slip and act in selfish, inconsiderate or hostile ways, you don't get to share the responsibility for what you do among others in the real world with active ingredients and outside agents in your head.

o   o   o

The quality of life is reduced when people concentrate upon interpretive labels for behavior. The fact is, labels foster the illusion of control.

"People occasionally stumble over the truth,
but most of them pick themselves up
and hurry off as if nothing had ever happened."

Winston Churchill

6

Emotions and Other Unicorns

Once you move your attention forward on your train of thought and action, ahead of the caboose to the cars that make up the body of the train, you are in for some fun. The habits of thinking and acting your mind has developed are the railroad cars.

Each of us has built habit upon habit throughout our lives to react to what the world sends our way. We develop most of our basic reactions to life situations as children—showing affection, feeling good about a compliment or approaching a tough job in a certain way. Our emotions capture the lion's share of attention when we use our minds. The following exercise will help to demonstrate that.

Settle your body comfortably, take a couple of deep breaths and then think of fairly recent events in your life when you were concerned about something. It could be a nettlesome situation at work, a financial concern or a personal worrisome incident.

Do your level best to recall the exact details of the situation, particularly where you were, what you saw, heard and especially how you felt.

Close your eyes and spend a few moments bringing the event back to life.

Now, set that experience aside, and get ready to locate a different one. This time you are seeking a moment when you were amused—it brought a chuckle. Recreate the situation exactly in your mind's eye. Pay attention to what you had to see, notice what you hear. Spend some time feeling the sensations related to the amusing moment. Close you eyes until you experience that moment fully again.

Set that one aside as well.

Next, try to remember what it is like to feel anxious. You could be sitting in the front seat of a roller coaster as it slowly climbs the first rise. The clacking noise of the wheels going over the tracks rings in your ears, and at the top you look down the hill, as the car hesitates before the plunge. Just be certain that when you settle back this time that you open your mind's eye onto a situation that produces an anxious reaction. Make it as real as possible.

Take a deep breath, and set the anxious response aside with the others. Now, recall a situation where you felt completely safe and at ease—a calm, peaceful or relaxed experience.

You may bring to mind a weekend morning when you find yourself half-awake in bed, familiar sounds of the house comforting you, but wanting to keep your eyes closed, your body still so you can enjoy the warmth. You can enjoy a detached feeling of comfort as if your body is more asleep than your head.

You may call on your own version of comfort and peace. But, as you close your eyes, be certain to do a detailed job of feeling every aspect of that comfy time again.

Now, set the secure sensation aside with the previous ones. Without hurrying, go over each one of the recalled experiences in the order you reconstructed them. Pay particular attention to *where* in your body you feel a specific sensation associated with a remembered incident most strongly.

It is odd for some people to discover that—whether the feeling is positive or negative, major or minor—it is registered first and foremost along the midline of your trunk. (If you didn't notice that, go over each situation again, reviving it as accurately as you can in every respect.)

The sensation you experience at your midline at various times during the day is a direct message from the major portion of your mind outside consciousness to the part of you that has been trained to talk about life. You can confirm again and again that when your mind wants to get your attention, rather than tapping you on the shoulder, you feel something along that midline of your chest.

Sometimes that feeling arises when you are anticipating something which you either dread or might find delightful. It turns up when you are experiencing a lustful moment, as well as one of revulsion. When you are filled with compassion, that feeling brings the message. And when you are startled, it is sharp. Have you ever noticed that it also turns up when you are at ease and comfortable?

In neurolinguistic programming jargon, that midline sensation is called "kinesthesia." I call it "that sensation." Call it anything you like, but familiarize yourself with it because that sensation is the signal that calls you to action every single time you respond emotionally or behaviorally to a situation. It is the engine on your train of thought and action.

If you wish to change, or improve your methods of interacting with real people in the real world, pay close attention to that midline sensation because every major response of yours begins with it.

Don't be concerned that this is turning into one of those "Get-in-touch with-your-feelings-and-tell-us-all-about-them" routines. The discipline I suggest you begin practicing runs on the exact opposite track.

Going back to the exercises you performed with that sensation, did you decide which portions of each each experience you would feel before you felt them, or did you notice them after you began? If you think about it, you will agree that all of them emerged first into your conscious awareness along with a feeling in your midline.

Is that sensation an emotion?

You may have already arrived at an answer and a decision that what we all call "emotions" are actually *Active Ingredients.* And just like other active ingredients such as quality, motivation or esteem, which are offered to us daily, they haven't got as much physical presence as an ordinary chair. It is clear now that what we call emotions are not the feelings in our bodies which precede them.

Emotional reactions are *not* feelings. When you fully appreciate this fact, you are well on the way to directing the powerful portion of your mind's repertoire of emotional habits of thinking and acting in new and more productive ways.

There are two extremes of kinesthesia like opposite poles—the Fight-or-Flight Response and the Relaxation Response. Both are opposing feelings inside your chest which can rise all the way up in your throat or sink all the way down to the pit of your stomach...or lower.

Your mind outside consciousness develops your emotional habits early. When you are safe, warm, full and dry as an infant, you feel the secure, relaxed sensation. You also model your parents' reactions to seeing their infant safe, warm, full and dry. Later you learn to call that acting "happy" or "satisfied" or "affectionate."

When you were an infant and felt yourself falling, or cold, wet and hungry, you switched to the opposite sensation along the midline and produced a noisy response behavior to accompany it. Soon you learned to mimic your parent's reactions to that display and associated the uncomfortable sensation with habits you later labeled as angry, lonely or sad.

Throughout your life, every day, thousands of reminders in your environment and in your memory simultaneously cue you to respond. Your mind signals you through the feeling that it is reacting. The stronger the fearful side of the feeling, the more your mind selects from patterns you've developed which we call "negative" emotions. If your mind signals with the comfortable sensation instead, you know that you are initiating a habitual reaction associated with more constructive emotional habits and their "positive" labels.

Emotions are habituated sets of thinking and acting which are executed fully outside your conscious reach, until you become aware of them emerging in your feelings, your thoughts and your behavior. Not all your habits are emotional ones. There are those you use to maintain your body. There are some simple social habits, like greeting, eating and parting. There are habits for functional processes like working, driving, and TV watching. Emotional habits are built the same, but tend to have more impact on us. I think of them as the cars on the train.

Because they are habitual, any attempt to improve a person's professional or personal performance by analyzing the origin of the response is ineffective. Try figuring out why you prefer blondes to brunettes. The person who realizes that the activities of the mind which are conscious can be directed consciously, and those which are *outside* consciousness must be directed differently, is a step ahead of the game.

In the next chapter, I am going to present you with methods to identify and redirect six of the most basic habits for thinking and acting.

But first, it is important to remember that most of your two-hundred million bits of activity each second are not formed into words, and aren't accessible to verbal guidance. Much of that activity is composed of disconnected images. A good deal of what goes on in your mind is registered in your conscious attention only as a dumb sensation with two sides—relaxed or awkward.

Second, it is important to remember that habits aren't conscious. You have no way of directly controlling which one you use at any given moment. If you dislike the way you express your emotional reactions in your professional and personal lives, you *can't* reach inside your mind and substitute a new one just by thinking you would like to. The only portion of an emotional reaction you can consciously manipulate fully is the label. And, as the tiger proved, labels aren't real life.

There is a portion of your emotional habits which you can consciously intervene upon, in an indirect fashion—the kinesthetic sensation along your midline. If you notice it as it is happening, and if you avoid automatically executing whatever habitual pattern is about to follow it, then you can interrupt the process.

By interrupting yourself at the moment you are experiencing the feeling, and at the beginning of an emotional response, you can create an environment for the portion of your mind outside consciousness to improve and update your repertoire.

As you know, you cannot *dictate* that process, but you can interrupt it as it happens, and improve your chances to develop a more effective response.

Since the whole process of mental, behavioral and emotional reactions is habitual and quick to emerge, you want to use something simple, but effective, to interrupt yourself at those moments when you catch yourself reacting in a fashion which you wish to improve. It will have to be something you can do during conversation—the majority of our responses, as well as our successes and failures, are expressed in the company of people. For that reason, you want a method which doesn't require so much inner talk that you lose track of the situation while you race to your caboose to try to improve performance outside your head.

So, what is simple, quick, pragmatic and doesn't require much verbiage?

Try exhaling. Sighing. Releasing a deep breath, slowly. That simple behavior interrupts almost every one of your emotional habits momentarily. Direct your mind to lean the way you wish it to, and quickly remove your attention from yourself and let it do its work by returning your conscious attention to the people around you.

Sighing at the moment you notice a feeling along the midline is something you can do anywhere. The hardest part is to *notice* that sensation and pay attention to it. We are constantly reminded by both intentional and subtle advertising that kinesthesia is something to *react* to, not something to attend to. When you begin practicing, within a short time you will be amazed at how often your mind has been giving you those little taps along the center of your body to notify you of its activity. Most of us ignore that feeling more often than we notice it. And fewer of us regard the feeling as a signal.

Just as kinesthetic sensation is a signal from your mind that a habit is about to appear on the scene of action, it can become a signal for you to interrupt that habit momentarily by sighing.

Once you do, you have to act fast, or your mind simply reverts to its old form. Remember that words cannot create behavioral patterns, but they always reinforce them and diminish those not associated with those particular words. By sighing at the moment you experience a midline sensation, you open a window of opportunity to guide your patterns in the most productive and beneficial direction. I suggest you repeat a simple, general phrase to yourself at that moment—something like: "I wonder how *well* I'll react, now?"

The most important portion of this process is what you do next. If you continue to monitor yourself, or worse, begin speculating about what kind of a response you consciously *wish* you'd produce, you will fail. You will actually end up reinforcing the very reaction habit you were trying to improve. That is why most group and individual efforts to improve emotional responses by talking at length about the nature of the *undesired* response hurt more than they help.

It is essential that once you notice the feeling, sigh to interrupt it, say your little piece to yourself and immediately direct your attention to the real world and the people around you. Focus immediately on any little aspect of your environment and do something to reinforce that. People now, plans later.

o   o   o

During private consults I help my clients with several approaches, among them hypnotherapy and neurolinguistic programming. One of my clients, Marge, needed assistance to overcome recurring pains from a back injury she received in an automobile accident two years earlier. Her story demonstrates how habitual patterns can be changed.

After exhausting physiological procedures, Marge's doctors prescribed biofeedback for pain on a regular basis and gave her Demerol so she could sleep. Marge had lived with a negative prognosis for more than a year when she came to me for counseling. After three sessions spread over several weeks, she improved somewhat, but still experienced nagging pains. I consulted with Dr. Dave Dobson about her and he suggested that when he worked with people who suffered lingering physical and emotional pain, he had noticed that most of his patients had never stopped steeling themselves against anticipated pain since the trauma had first occurred. Acting apprehensively kept the pain alive. For some people, my colleague suggested, the apprehensive habit doesn't get shut off and by constantly preparing the body for injury the mind continues to reinforce the experience of getting hurt over and over again. The person revives a memory of pain long after the physiological cause for the pain had been eliminated.

Once I knew I had Marge's full attention in our next session, I made sure she brought the recurrent discomfort of the old injury to the front of her mind, then interrupted her train of thought by telling her a story about my father who was an executive for a chain of retail stores. I told her that one night he was called to one of the branches of his company which had been burglarized. He was the only person the police could locate who had a key to the store. The alarm was still ringing shrilly when he arrived to shut it off and assist the police. It was so loud people couldn't hear each other talk. The irritating noise had continued unnecessarily—the burglars were long gone. The alarm was no longer needed.

Marge's mind was working just like that burglar alarm, sending out signals of danger long after the crisis was over. I rehearsed with her how to interrupt that anticipatory habit by sighing at certain points while telling her the alarm story. Her mind caught on. Within six months Marge was declared fully fit to return to her physically demanding job by the company's own doctors. But that wasn't the last time I saw her professionally. About a year later, she consulted me about another situation. She had been diagnosed the previous day with a serious condition in one breast and immediate surgery had been recommended. Marge asked her doctor how much time she had to find an alternative to surgery. He gave her less than two months and at the same time warned her emphatically that he would not take responsibility for her case unless she followed his urgent recommendation—surgery—the next day.

I looked at her and asked if I was her chosen alternative. To my question of what she expected me to do, she replied maddeningly, "You know—whatever you do."

My work with her started right there and then. (Much of what I did is outlined in the last section of this book.) When she was relaxed I began talking about several things. I talked about how as children we did most of our physical growing at night while we were sleeping, and how as adults we still do a lot of changing and growing in the depth of sleep.

I told her how our minds outside consciousness do fascinating things: we wake up before the alarm goes off; we select and digest our food; we can lower and raise our blood pressure, we can build new cells and are able to select and discard old ones.

I described at length the inner workings of this process. I asked her to imagine being inside herself looking at healthy, new cells and selecting old, used-up, waste ones to toss out. I asked her to envision a faucet turning off the blood supply to old cells, watching them shrivel up and then have her replace them with brand, new healthy clones.

I also mentioned the function of any bathroom where eventually most old cells make their final exit from our lives. I then suggested that she remember the idea of old cells departing whenever she heard a sound of water rushing—the moment which usually heralds the final exit of waste. When my work had ended, hers began. Again, she was successful. Several weeks later, Marge's surgery was postponed indefinitely since all evidence of trouble had disappeared. Years later, healthy and happy, Marge was married. I just heard she is expecting her first child.

From my association with Dr. Dave Dobson, I learned to hold people's habits of thinking in high regard. Although these habits take place substantially outside conscious reach, and are not in the form of words for the most part, these habitual traits of life experiences are much closer to the front of people's trains of thought and action than any conscious commentary. Habits are much more influential on our actions than any verbal display, and manifest themselves in the quality of life we are leading.

These habits are so potent that the late Milton Erickson, widely regarded as one of the finest practitioners of hypnotherapy, said, "The first job of the therapist is to interrupt the limiting mind set of the client." When Erickson or Dobson discuss the thinking process, it is primarily about what takes place without spoken words, outside conscious reach.

It is helpful to remember that my client's pain as well as her problem cells were produced and maintained with the aid of her habits of thought. It wasn't necessary for Marge to understand what they meant, where they came from, or how long she'd had them. I didn't understand, either. What I was called upon to do was to interrupt the old habits, and invite Marge to substitute new productive ones at each opportunity.

Habits are habits. Your mind uses those you reinforce.

Thinking habits are learned much more easily if you avoid specific, verbal directions. Using stories, implications and deletions (making certain things more obvious by their omission) are effective methods to help change ineffective and destructive thinking habits. That's why I never actually identified the sound she heard upon leaving the bathroom.

I had made use of another observation about Marge. When I first met her, she introduced herself as a "brawny sailing woman." Taking into account that she was no taller than five-foot-one and that her previous job was in a totally male-dominated, manual labor-intensive industry, I picked up on the habitual defiance in her thinking about male and female stereotypes. I made use of that bit of knowledge.

As she was about to leave my office after our last session, I said quickly, "Now, don't get your hopes up too high. This kind of an approach has been quite successful in the past, but each of us has his limits and we have to live with them. If you were a *man,* you could probably do this standing on your head, but since you're only a woman, don't expect too much".

She clenched her fists as she rose halfway from the chair, then she shook her finger at me and with a grin on her face said, "Oh, no, I know what you're trying to do."

Unknown to Marge (until now) her other fist stayed clenched as the brawny sailing woman took her old cells out of my office, and out of her life.

o   o   o

For those of you who are wondering about the value and application of the technique I used with Marge and the idea of sighing as well, remember that the mind responds much more readily to direction, than to dictation. The success or failure in human interaction requires more attention to others than to your own thinking. And, most importantly, remember that you didn't build your emotional habits by conscious means. If you wish to update some of those old habits to meet your present professional and personal needs, you will be more successful by using brain-friendly, rather than brain-antagonistic means.

Sit down with some paper and make a list of several situations where you've experienced a setback caused by an emotional habit.

I did some telemarketing several years ago, and discovered several aspects of the sales business which were adversely affected by certain emotional reactions. Rejection is one of the negative experiences in selling, and there is always more than one choice on how to approach the work load. One can either act upset and frustrated or act overly enthusiastic or optimistic about results. Acting angry or bored, acting too casual or detached are pitfalls any telemarketer or salesperson will tell you are professional hazards. Wouldn't you like to catch those kind of reactions and set them aside at the moment they began?

Maybe you'd prefer to practice at home. Can you list a few upcoming moments in which you will want to notice that special feeling emerging from behind your sternum? How about doing or assigning chores, responding with affection, or responding *to* affection? What kind of trouble can predictable moments of acting bored, distracted, unhappy, lonely, guilty, self-conscious or worried cause you? Where would you like to implement your well-worn habits for acting enthused, loving, playful, sensitive or passionate?

Pick several specific times at work in which you are fairly certain you will get a chance to redirect an old emotional habit, and jot down a reminder about each one for yourself. Do the same with several situations you've been reacting to in less-than-elegant ways. Each day, select one from each list to keep near the front of your mind, and pay attention to the chances your mind offers you to make improvements. Remember, this is all about "when"—not "why." Avoid the temptation to plan a different response. Just focus on when you know one would be helpful.

You will find yourself acting as if you actually trusted that part of your mind which constructed your response patterns and reinforced them in the first place. You will be attending to—and offering some direction for—the part of your mind that selects all the cars of thinking and acting on your train of thought. But then which part of your mind is more important—that selector part, or the Pez dispenser in your caboose?

Adopting this new habit of directing rather than recapitulating our emotional reactions brings two other major benefits. You will blow apart the myth about emotions carried on every pop radio station, in every romance novel, in every psychology text, and in most bedrooms and kitchens across America. You need not be filled with, overwhelmed by, carried away by, destroyed by, burned up by, held back by, undercut by, pressured by, stressed over, distracted by, disturbed by, or disappointed by a thing which isn't there, ever again. If you are, you will know it is with your own cooperation.

The second benefit is that you will be able to take a more active role in actually improving your responses to people and the world, rather than simply buying better and better definitions for why you haven't done so up till now.

How do you feel about that?

o   o   o

Emotions are not feelings, but habits of thought and action cued to begin by a physical sensation.

7

Building an Onion

So far in this book, I hope you've been able to appreciate how the mind associates words with experiences and does it in multiple combinations, reinforcing those associations along the way. Also, you understand how emotional reactions work. You know the difference between actual feelings and the habits of thoughts and action which a feeling predicts.

Just as there is a difference between a feeling and an emotional reaction, there is a difference between what we label as attitudes, mind sets, beliefs or values and the unique experiences those labels attempt to capture. This middle section in the book addresses those thinking habits you have developed which reinforce your particular perception of the world. Those habits of thinking are expressed much more by *how* you do and say things than by *what* is said. For example, while American business spends a great deal of money to improve human resources by empowering employees, when the time comes to implement "people first" policies and procedures, most managers leave their seminar workbooks on the shelf and manage with their customary tool: threat of dismissal. Old habits of thinking or mind sets are not the team-building or the care for "our company family" approach, but remain the authoritarian and prescriptive methods.

When the pressure is on, which we experience as that kinesthetic sensation along our midline, we are driven toward the familiar, *not* the new and spontaneous. The most familiar reactions are those which are habitual and unthinking.

That is why employees who attend team-building seminars for empowerment see themselves with precious little power when it comes down to putting into practice what they learn in class. *When creatures of habit confront conscious intentions, their habits usually prevail.*

We are all biased by our experiences. We spend a lot of time seeking confirmation or reassurances from other people that the model of the world we've constructed is a "good," "appropriate" or "valuable" model to have. We fight over discrepancies between our world views. We fall in love with people who have constructed similar perceptions. We go to classes to learn to deal with people who have opposing views. And if that doesn't work, we just fire them. The only thing we are *not* taught to do very well is to build a different, more varied model by directing the mind in ways that respect the way it functions. We talk about tolerance while rewarding conformity.

By our tenth birthday, we have formed basic habits of thought and action which we repeat dependably in all similar situations. This process happens by reinforcement, by conditioning from other people and by our own input. Words are the last part of the process, and serve mainly to reinforce patterns and habits which are already in place.

Remember Fred, the employee I was asked to help overcome rude and pretentious behavior in Chapter One?

I was discussing this case with an organizational development consultant from New York City. He was quick to advertise his own habits of thought by telling me that there was only one way to deal with such a man. "It's obvious that he uses big words to keep people at arm's length because of his insecurities. My solution would be to confront him with his behavior and get him to understand why he's acted so rudely in the past."

I thought that was a terrible idea.

Put yourself in Fred's shoes for a minute. Consider that the man never *decided* to cover his alleged insecurities by consciously building a big vocabulary. Also, what would it be like to hear a very important consultant tell you that basically you act overly important because you are insecure. Afterwards, every time you approach a fellow employee you must be conscious of your insecurity so you can *tell* yourself to act differently.

The point of this is that *Goal-Setting* for personal performance is not brain-friendly. If you spend your time making elaborate plans and setting specific goals for how you will act, think and feel in the future, you will eventually have to confront the simple fact that you will fail. Everybody tends to respond the way they've practiced responding, no matter how many times they consciously wish differently. Setting performance goals may actually *reinforce* old response patterns. You don't know what it is going to be like a few miles down the tracks. You haven't been there before. You can't predict the outcome, nor control the process of human interaction.

Likewise, *Numerical Ratings* of primate performance are not brain-friendly. Tests, quizzes, surveys, numerical performance evaluations, or any quantitative attempts to direct your mind's habits simply provide you with more of the status quo, with the additional bonus of discomfort or fear. You did not form, nor do you reinforce your habits of thought and action by listing fifteen pros and cons in your head. Habits, by definition, happen whether you understand them or not. Think about your mind. Why does it like the things it likes? What's your favorite ice cream, music or sexual preference? Why does your mind dislike things in the way that it dislikes them? What's your favorite race, religion or political movement? Why do you do the things you do? Why do you not do the things you don't do?

The meanest habit of thinking most unprotected consumers have bought into repeatedly is the one that implies that your mind must be consciously *told* to do something. But you *can* direct your mind to lean in different, more constructive ways at the very moments you are heading in a direction you no longer wish to follow. You cannot peel the onion, but you can build a new one. You *can* encourage your mind outside consciousness to reinforce habits other than the ones you presently use by attending to the signs of those habits and redirecting these signs whenever you notice them pointing down a track you've already travelled and no longer wish to follow.

These signs are implicit in your speech, between-the-lines. They reveal whole sections of your mind's presumptions about the world, yourself and other people. These presumptions are based upon your own experiences and not upon somebody else's ideas. It is the dynamic between ideas and action which holds the hope of improving your life's quality.

A classic study in performance improvement demonstrates this. Three groups of basketball players were involved. One group practiced playing as usual. Another group practiced the same amount of time, only they practiced in their heads. The third group spent time actually playing the game and then going through the play again, but this time in their heads. The third group spent more time with their game than the other two groups. The first two groups progressed at about the same rate. It was the third group that directed their actions on the court as well as in their minds which progressed more rapidly.

Research shows that America's children are practicing habits of thinking at an early age which destroy their chances of progressing beyond a certain point scholastically, and consequently in their adult lives. We have built a world where our children are like the second group of basketball players. They sit in front of the TV, but they neglect to practice actually *doing* anything about learning.

Big Bird cannot write complete sentences for our kids, nor can he practice making change for them, or teach them to hold a complex set of presumptions in their heads to enable them to appreciate literature or a formal set of instructions. These mental habits leave less than half of our graduating high school seniors able to make change for a two-item purchase at McDonalds and unable to write a comprehensible sentence in English.

These young people have reinforced habits of thought and action which emphasize immediate gratification, simplistic answers to complicated problems, and a disrespect for other people. The neuroscientists suggest that this is not a situation easily corrected at a later age.

The saying "Use it, or lose it" certainly holds true. It turns out that, although we can direct our minds to lean in the direction of new habits of thinking at any age, the actual physical structure of the brain is affected by how we use the mind. The more we exercise a portion of our brain, the more complex and efficient its connections become. The less we use it, the fewer the connections. In childhood, there are periods of time when whole sections of the brain are more ripe to be developed than at any other time during life. We can still do it later—it's just harder. Think about the "brawny sailing woman" I introduced earlier. Do you remember that as I worked with her, I did not tell her how to think or act differently? I suggested things, I intimated others, and I used stories to send the message. I implied all the important parts. She *acted* in ways that accommodated those implications, and as a consequence, reinforced an entirely different set of habits in her own way of thinking.

We can advance quickly by appreciating and redirecting a limiting habit in our thinking. We risk backsliding when we try to just substitute a new phrase for the old habit.

When I was working in the field of alcohol and drug rehabilitation as a family therapist, I encountered a young woman and her mother. The girl was about sixteen, and had a brief, but intense history of using pot excessively and behaving in an equally damaging manner with young men.

Mother and daughter sat across from each other in the circle of our counseling group of about thirty-five people. The young woman said to her mother, "My issue with you is that you never say you love me." Most parents of teenagers will agree that this is not an unusual remark. But the mother's answer, which launched me into action, was certainly not typical. She said, "I know—and let me tell you why."

Before the older woman could continue, I quickly placed myself between them, facing the daughter, with my back to the mother. I turned my head and asked the mother to give me a moment, then I asked the daughter to close her eyes and relive as many of the most intensely pleasurable experiences she could recall when she smoked pot. I encouraged her to see, hear, feel and smell every single detail.

When I was satisfied that she was actually reliving the sensations of pot use and the responses she'd rehearsed and associated with it, I placed my hand on her shoulder, and told her to hold on to those impressions a little while longer. At the same time, I moved to stand at her side, revealing her to her mother.

Holding on to her shoulder, I told her to open her eyes, and I said to her mother: "Look her in the eye and tell her you love her, if you really mean it."

Finally, the older woman said quietly, "I love you," I held fast to the girl's shoulder and asked the mother to repeat it. She did as I requested. After she said the words to her child several more times, I let go of the girl's shoulder.

The daughter slowly refocused her eyes on her mother's face and repeated the mother's phrase. A little while later, after chatting with mother and daughter, my supervisor excused them from any more family group, indicating that any more verbal digging into their history would only cause trouble, not cure it. From observing them, he told them he felt they had accomplished what they had come to do.

You may have noticed that I never said a word during that entire period about what was being substituting for what, who had compensated for whom, what was missing and what needed replacing. I simply *inferred* by deed and implication that different and pleasant associations were about to be made. I treated it dramatically and seriously.

The only thing the mind will not do is stop making connections. It reinforces, associates and selects for repetition your habits of thinking, feeling and action on a twenty-four hour basis. If you are willing to take advantage of this fact, you can attend to your own implications, and practice interrupting and redirecting them as they emerge in your speech and between-the-lines.

The changes that occur are not as instantaneous as those demonstrated in the previous anecdote, although one would be well-advised not to rule out that possibility. But we must accommodate our mind and respect the way it functions. Habits take time to build. Give up the old, best-selling notion that simplistic language helps us break habits. It doesn't. Begin using language in provocative, far-reaching ways. Instead of goal and deadline thinking, what would happen if we began implying that our world was filled with starting lines? Wouldn't that point us to more interactions with other people who are the arbiters of our personal and professional success?

Repeating happy phrases in our heads won't do. We have to attend to the biases that make us unique as they are expressed between the lines in what we imply about the world as we experience it. Everyone is biased. Everyone has expectations about the outcomes for every situation. Everyone is prejudiced by the life she has lived and the habits of thinking and reaction that life has reinforced. We are biased by the way we associate words with experiences in our heads.

The only thing we need give up in order to redirect our habits of thought is the presumption that ours alone are the right biases, prejudices,and expectations. There may be an objective "right" ocean out there, but you or I will never know because we each have different "oceans" in our heads. Just like everybody else.

Following are six exercises. They are similar to the one you used for habitual emotional situations. Their purpose is to help you avoid getting hooked into inner dialogue—which are conversations that you can never win. The only real difference between these exercises and the ones you've done before is that each of the six categories of "implication" you are about to explore provide you with a different phrase to say. These phrases are designed to counter the limiting presumption that you can talk your mind into reacting by consciously understanding it.

Please remember that if you find yourself continuing to discuss life in your head after having done one of the six exercises (interventions), you are not doing it well. If you are wondering about what you meant, why you said this or that, why you picked the phrases you did, and similar ramblings, you have just reinforced the mind games the why merchants would like you to play.

These exercises are designed to *minimize* your conscious inner dialogue—to help you stop talking to yourself and playing with repetitive thoughts like a squirrel running on a treadmill in a cage. If you find yourself talking to yourself at the end of each exercise, then go back and start over again.

On a piece of paper write down two or three sentences in answer to each of the following:

1. Name a favorite person or situation and how you know that it is a favorite one.

2. Name a least favorite person or situation and how you know that is a least favorite one.

3. Name something about yourself that you wish to change and how you know that you wish to change it.

4. Name something about yourself that you wish to keep the same and how you know that you wish to keep it.

If you have access to a video camera, then film yourself reading the answers. If not, a mirror will do nicely.

Okay, read your first answer from above and examine how you have expressed it. It might occur to you to ask: "Who is the **Active Party?**"

Implied between the lines of most every statement we make about our lives is the source of what is happening, the who-or-what's-in-charge. Now, compare your questions and answers and ask yourself who (or what) the active party is in each one. There can only be one of two choices in every circumstance: Either the person talking is the **Active Party**—she is doing things that affect the world, or the person talking is implying that the world is the **Active Party**—it is doing things to her. For example:

1. "My favorite situation is my job. It's the one thing I can always count on to challenge me to help build my self-esteem. Because my work deals with people, every situation is different, which makes me more creative."

2. "I love my job. I wake up every day and drive to work anticipating how I'm going to rise to the day's challenges. I have a chance to exercise my ability to act creatively on a daily basis, because I'm constantly dealing with different people."

Did you recognize in example number one that the world, in this case the job, was the **Active Party,** providing the speaker with a "thing which offers challenges and self-esteem" and makes the speaker "more creative"?

By contrast, in example number two, although the subject and some of the words are identical to the first one, the speaker is the one acting on the job by "waking, anticipating and driving," as well as "acting creatively" as she "deals with people." In example one, it is the *job* which is characterized as "dealing with people."

There are several ways to notice these implications. For those of you skilled in grammar, the active and passive voice and transitive and intransitive verbs give them away. In business jargon, you could seek the **proactive** or **reactive** person. Or, you can simply ask yourself, "Who's really doing what to whom?"

If I love something, then I am the active party. If something makes me love it, or I am swept away, overwhelmed or filled with love, then the world ("love") is the **Active Party**. If I have a temper, then the temper acts on me. If I act mad, then I am doing the acting. If I feel a pain in my shoulder, then I am doing the feeling. If she gives me a pain in the neck, then she's acting on me. Take a moment or two and read your first answer into the mirror. Do it twice. If you have it on tape, run the tape a couple of times. Now ask yourself: Who's the **Active Party** between the lines of those statements? Is it you acting on the world, or is it the other way around?

In doing this exercise with many people, I have yet to find an exception. There is always an **Active Party** implied. Remember, you cannot answer this question completely, nor can you answer it incorrectly. The point is to notice what mind set you reveal as you discuss a favorite person or situation when it comes to the **Active Party**.

Now read the second answer into the mirror. Some—but not all—of the people I work with detect that the **Active Party** shifts when moving from a favorite to a less-favorite subject. Others represent themselves as the **Active Party** in both cases, while others emerge as being the party acted upon in both cases.

Remember, the temptation will be for you to stop and speculate about "whys" and "wherefores" when these exercises are intended to help you do exactly the opposite: notice how you have just implied the direction of your world, and to redirect that implication if you wish. Internal discussion is not necessary.

Once you've determined which the **Active Party** was in your first answer, take a deep breath, and rephrase it so that the opposite is true. Do the same with your second statement. If you were acting upon the world, then sigh, and re-state the same thing, only this time as if the world is acting upon you. Notice the differences in how you respond to these changes.

Think, for instance, of a situation when you want to represent yourself as the party being acted *upon* by the world. As a subject to be acted upon, sex usually comes up first in the groups

I've worked with. But what about other pleasant situations? Would you rather perceive yourself as being the active party, or the reactive one? What about painful situations? What about work? Are you required to *always* be the proactive party? In much of management training, being the **Active Party** is glorified by the very same people who extol the virtues of good listeners and the exceptional qualities of natural communicators.

You will find that there truly is no right answer to which way to characterize your habits of thinking at the level of the **Active Party**. Sometimes you will perceive yourself as the one acting on (others and the world). Other times, it is more beneficial for you to be acted upon (by others or the world). Which way do you wish your habits to lean? Which direction would you like to take? If you attend to your experience in the moment, the direction will be clear.

Here is one more example to clarify things fully before moving on. In my private consults, I have often encountered people who said they were acted upon by things like depression, anxiety, stress and various other influences.

Say the following two phrases slowly to yourself, and take note which feels less or more comfortable. Close your eyes if you wish.

1. I suffer from a depression.
2. Sometimes, I act depressed.

Which phrase do you perceive as more likely to be changed in the future? Which is less likely?

One of the most important areas in which to practice this first method of redirecting your thinking habits is in the area of emotional reactions. Be certain during the next few weeks of practicing with this **Active Party** tool that you characterize your emotional reactions as what they really are. Unless you wish to live in a world where emotions can strike you down like misguided lightning, you will be cautious about your thinking habits. Just listen to love songs on the radio for a while, and you'll hear exactly how to always represent yourself as acted *upon* by emotions, never building a sense of your own ability to direct your emotional reactions (there are no "emotions").

Now that you have the format for redirecting all six categories of mental implication, you can investigate them one by one as they follow.

Refer to one of them, like the **Active Party** by asking yourself the suggested question, sigh to interrupt the current habit, and, if you wish to alter your presumption about your world, rephrase it immediately to imply the opposite habit of thought. There will always be only two choices—it is always one way or the other.

As in the emotional reaction practice, the last step is the most crucial one. Once you've sighed and rephrased your remarks, get your mind out of your head and immediately back into the world.

The second category for switching implications in your habits of thought is time.

Ask yourself, "Is it **Moving, or Stuck?**"

Here are two examples:

1. "I want always to keep my sense of humor. All my life, people have told me that I make them laugh, and I hope that stays the same in the future."

2. "Something I want to change about myself is my sense of humor. Everything is always funny to me and I don't take things as seriously as I should ."

Can you recognize that in the first example, time is represented as in motion, with a discernable past, present and future? In example number two, everything is characterized in the present tense, as if the speaker were stuck in a never-ending moment without a yesterday or tomorrow. Which way would you prefer to perceive the different times in your life? Did you answer "It depends?"— because it does. Would you rather be adrift on a passionate wave or experiencing a few minutes of really great sex? Do you wish to perceive yourself as someone who is clumsy, inadequate and inefficient, or as someone who has been learning the hard way to overcome obstacles on the road to present accomplishments? Remember that these types of **Moving** or **Stuck** time associations are reinforced outside consciousness more powerfully than spoken words, because they are implied.

Read another answer from your paper into the mirror, or from the tape. Play it again, and pick out whether you have represented everything described as existing only in the present (**Stuck**) or if you've included the passing of time in your descriptions (**Moving**).

I have had clients who discovered an odd thing about their personal habits of thought. They talk about what they want for themselves as being in the future, while simultaneously discussing what they don't want (failures, character flaws, mistakes) in the present tense only. Imagine how the mind is required to reinforce that situation:

"What I want is somewhere ahead of me, while what I don't want always seems to be here now."

Painful situations are the ones which you want to represent as moving through time, while there is no law against reinforcing pleasurable moments as stuck in the present. If you are aiming at future achievements, be careful about reinforcing a *someday, but never today* bias between the lines. Link the accomplishments to both past and future, so that you associate moving toward things with those you've already reached and outgrown.

One more example might help. Early in my work I counseled a woman client who complained of headaches. She told me, "I want you to know I've tried self-hypnosis and it doesn't work."

I asked how she had drawn that conclusion about self-hypnosis.

"I went to someone who told me to close my eyes, see myself in a field, relax my body and say things to make my headaches go away, and it didn't work," she replied.

"What did you say to yourself?" I asked.

It turned out that she had repeated the following affirmation to herself: "I don't have a headache, I don't have a headache, I don't have a headache."

"Did you have a headache at the time?" I asked.

She answered, "Yes."

I asked, "Who did you think you were fooling?"

I went on to point out she could have said all sorts of things like, "I wonder how soon I'll feel more comfortable" or "I wonder when this pain will be behind me." If you attend closely to the ways she represented time as **Stuck** while I encouraged her to get it **Moving**, you can make some connections for yourself.

Read a few more of your answers and notice any shifts in the implications about time until you are comfortable recognizing them. Then, read one, sigh to interrupt the habit, and quickly rephrase it to present the opposite implication.

Do this several times and remember the final step. Once you've rephrased a statement's implicit suggestions, it is essential to get your mind focused on any little thing in your immediate environment to distract your conscious attention from the inner process of your mind long enough to let it work.

The third category question is, "**In Body,** or **In Head**?"

This implication has a little more to do with behavior and

requires more observation of your demeanor and your voice as you read your responses. It is the simplest to notice, but often the most challenging to alter. It can be revolutionary to your ability to enjoy life's pleasures as well as to endure life's discomforts.

Read both a favorite response and least favorite response and watch and listen to yourself very carefully. It would be most helpful if you had someone to do the observing for you, because some of us are poor observers of our own performances.

As you read your answers, did you notice whether or not you were animated in your delivery? What happened with the tone and volume of your voice? Did your face move? Did you gesture, did you move your body ?

Or were you still, using little animation, and speaking in a regular, monotone voice? If you're not sure, do it again. If you still can't tell, it's time to resort to commercial TV. Pick out a talk show, or a panel news discussion and watch and listen for these distinctions. It won't take long for you to notice them. Return to the mirror, and pay attention—with those other examples fresh in your mind. You *will* begin to sort out distinctions. And, they will fall into the **In Body,** or **In Head** category.

What you have observed is referred to as "association" or "disassociation".

During one of my seminars in Detroit, a man stood in front of the group and read all four of his responses while being taped.

He was astonished to discover that when he discussed his least favorite situation and the parts of his performance he liked the least, he was very animated. He moved as he spoke and his voice was quite expressive whenever he commented on what he *disliked* about his life.

When his attention turned to what he wanted *more* of, and what portions of his life he thoroughly enjoyed, he appeared to be stuck in suspended animation—like an ant caught in a chunk of amber—his body and voice were frozen.

Recently, something similar happened during a program in Pittsburgh. A woman participant described her least favorite person by bending almost double, raising her arms out from her sides as she pulled herself up to her full height, got redder and redder in the face and roared, "Because he just makes my blood boil!"

By contrast, she discussed her most favorite person in a soft, even tone while she leaned relaxed against a counter, moving only her eyebrows and lips.

Can you guess what characteristics indicate **In Body** or **In Head**? The discovery the man in Detroit made, as he later described it to me, was realizing how clearly he had reinforced all the actions and sensations associated with what he *didn't* want in his life while never rehearsing and reinforcing actions and sensations (and more productive mind sets) associated with what he wanted. His wife watched the tape and he enlisted her help in reminding him to sigh and "replay" his future statements to meet his needs of what he wanted.

This one implication, handled well, can alleviate untold numbers of what the experts call "stress-related dysfunctions." Remember, NLP reminded us the mind and body are a connected system; what happens in one impacts the other. Also, remember that you get what you rehearse, *regardless* of what you intend.

Doctors Larry Dossey and Bernie Siegel—among others—point out at least one fact about physical health which makes this section of special interest to those who want to live longer.

The top indicators for heart disease are high blood pressure, high cholesterol, smoking and diabetes. Nobody can accurately predict when a first heart attack might happen. Siegel and

Dossey point out that there is reliable data to support the fact that a *psychological* factor, such as "Job Dissatisfaction," is a more accurate predictor of first attacks than any physical symptom. When we couple these studies with several others there comes to light an astonishing fact. Human primates are the only animals on earth which reinforce death by heart attacks at one specific hour of the week more than any other hour. That hour is nine o'clock on Monday morning. That could make us quite curious about what habits we rehearse **In our Body** and which ones we rehearse **In our Head**. Perhaps some adjustments are in order.

The next category of thinking habits can be explored by asking the question, "**Scarcity** or **Possibility**?"

Here are a couple of examples:

1. "My favorite thing is going to the movies. I wish I could go more often, because that's the only place I'm really happy."

2. "One of my favorite things is going to the movies. Every time I go I can't predict just how much I'll enjoy it. I wonder how soon I will be able to go again."

Most people find this easiest category in which to notice their own implied habits of thought. If you recognized the first example of "only one favorite" thing —often sought but rarely experienced—and the *only* chance for experiencing real happiness as an example of **Scarcity** thinking, then you are on the appropriate track.

Example number two demonstrates **Possibility** by implying more than one favorite thing, which is always unpredictable, and happening again soon, even though "soon" isn't defined. Now that you are prepared, you are ready to read through your own examples.

Go over two or three of your answers and check where the possibilities are implied, and where the limitations or scarcities are invoked.

Again, as in all these categories, there is no right time or wrong time to reinforce either side of a category. There is only the type of mind set you wish to reinforce at a specific time. Common sense dictates that if you wish to heighten your successes, characterizing them as "rare, unapproachable, unlikely, difficult, or almost impossible" is sure to bring **Scarcity** to mind.

On the other hand, are you like some people I've worked with who insisted on characterizing all future endeavors as "fraught with dangers, having lots of downsides, very risky, and probably something I'll live to regret?" These kind of **Possibilities** most brains can live *without* reinforcing.

Remember that in using these tools in real life, you want to notice which way you have implied that the world "is" for your mind. If you want to change direction, just sigh, rephrase your statements to imply the alternative in that category, and immediately move your attention to something else that will distract you. Less talk, more interaction.

If the terms **Possibility** and **Scarcity** are familiar, please avoid taking them as a license to resort to hours of conscious affirmations or goal-setting. The implications of just reframing your original statement and leaving your mind to work as it always has; reinforcing those habits of thought serves you much more profitably.

Speaking of profit, listen to any news broadcast regarding the economy, the markets or financial news in general if you want to hear plenty of examples of **Scarcity** and **Possibility** thinking. You will find the majority leaning strongly toward one side over the other.

The fifth category for inviting your mind to reinforce habits of thinking is answered by the one-word question, "**Metaphor**?" You want to find the story being told about your version of the world between the lines of your statements. Believe it or not, there is almost *always* a metaphoric word or phrase in even the shortest remarks.

Consider the metaphors which have appeared so far. What about "boiling blood?" Does it really boil, and does that mean that she "gets hot" around him? How can a whole person be a "pain in your neck?" What type of mortar does one use to "build a self-esteem?" Is total effort implied by "rising to challenges" and "exercising abilities?" What causes someone to have "job satisfaction?" What exactly is a "passionate wave?"

When you get right down to it, what exactly are comfort or pain, if not metaphors for associations behind the scenes of consciousness in the speaker's mind? Each descriptive word tells a story, particularly in the ear (and mind) of the speaker. The question "**Metaphor?**" is aimed to help you check periodically that the story you've just reinforced is truly the one you wish to be reinforcing millions of times per second outside your conscious reach.

"That just kills me," you might say, or "Stop, I can't stand it." "This is murder" also comes to mind. "It's an uphill battle," "The worst is yet to come," and "Between a rock and a hard place" are life stories you may wish to avoid.

Read through your answers again now, and find out how many one-word, or metaphoric phrases you can unearth from between the lines.

You might find it interesting to note that as a culture, unprotected consumers have bought prevailing metaphors which are most commonly used to describe various institutions in American life. For example, can you guess the current, prevailing cultural metaphor for "business?" If you said "war" or "warfare," thump yourself on the back.

"It's an uphill battle" is just the start. What about other implications like, "Attacking the market aggressively," "Targeting our market," "Marshalling our resources," "Launching our campaign," "Revising our strategy," "Applying more offensive tactics," "Eliminating or wiping-out the competition," "Fighting for our lives," "Battling, fighting, scratching and clawing your way to the top," as well as "achieving our objectives."

Bearing in mind that we are creatures of habit, can you guess what our current prevailing metaphor for "sports" is? That's right—it is "warfare" again. How about our metaphor for "medicine?" If we're collecting arrays of chemical and surgical weapons to attack invading sources of infection and drive them from the body, so the brave little soldier (patient) can win his fight against disease, I guess we are still at "war."

What about "relationships?" Shucks, that would be the "battle of the sexes," wouldn't it? Well, what about education? Nope, we're all busy "fighting against illiteracy," aren't we? Ditto for "politics" or "government," "religion" and many other institutions. It seems this "warfare" metaphor gets little rest in our culture.

I wonder occasionally how people can actually act surprised when they watch the rising tides of violence around us and ask where it could possibly be coming from. You may not get exactly what you wish or pray for, but you will find your mind reinforcing the world model right behind your eyes. So, be very careful about the stories you imply, or they might just jump up and bite you.

The last category is revealed in another one-word question, which is "**Judgment?**" What makes this category a bit different is that there is *always* judgment reflected in any remark you or anyone else makes in regard to experiences. The question is designed to remind you of this fact and to help you remember you can redirect any implied judgment along different lines, but you cannot eliminate it.

When you think about it for a moment, you will recognize that in each of the categories you've actually isolated a particular portion of how you "judge" the world to be. If you recall that no one else has the same associations for the world which you have reinforced, you can see how these judgments could be perceived by someone else as biases, values, beliefs or even prejudices.

There are more obvious implications of judgment available for you to steer in directions you wish your mind to travel more frequently. The most obvious one is the implication of "right" and "wrong" in everyday remarks. "That's good," you might say, or, "That's not right at all."

There are second-cousin phrases which go with right and wrong. Comparative terms like "better" and "worse" are also close relations to the "Good/Bad," "Right/Wrong" family of implications. Finally, there are universal quantifiers like: "totally, everyone, always, never, ever, completely, absolutely, invariably or nobody," and operators like "should, have to, must, gotta, or ought to!"

By themselves, these are just words, but in combination with other words they hint at your version of the world and amount to direct judgments about what is good and what is bad about that world.

What makes this possibly the most critical category for you to practice recognizing and rerouting is the talent your mind has for reinforcing implications at an incredibly fast and massive rate. You know that any word brings all associated experiences (ocean) closer to the "front" of your mind, as it reinforces them all again. You know the process actively diminishes other unrelated experiences from being drawn upon—even if they would help. You know that you can't stop that process from happening.

These "Right/Wrong, Good/Bad" associations are some of the oldest and strongest in your head. They were used, among others things, to toilet train you. The uncritical nature of your mind in early childhood, the judgmental implications which eventually harken back to "Good Boy!" and "Bad Girl!" remain powerful influences on your habits for feeling, thinking and acting.

To avoid dredging up pre-juvenile associations with such force that they inevitably reinforce childish habits of thought and action, the simplest method is to remember to interrupt and rephrase any statement which contains the words good, bad, right, wrong, better, worst, have to, got to, should, always, never, and so forth.

You would be astonished to discover how many sophisticated people still resort to harsh "good girl, bad boy" inner dialogues, reinforcing the terrors of childhood in an effort to motivate themselves. The irony is that they are using implications which are virtually guaranteed to have them feeling, thinking and reacting in old habitual ways while attempting to guide themselves into new and different responses. Maybe they can start on a couple of new onions, soon.

Run through your comments one more time, and listen carefully between the lines for traces of these judgmental implications. You will find them.

Notice how each category can also carry a judgment about the "rightness" or "wrongness" of the words being expressed.

Active Party: "We are all victims."

Stuck or **Moving**: "This can't go on much longer."

In Body or **Head**: "This is totally hopeless!" (Arms thrown in the air.)

Scarcity or **Possibility**: "We're just about out of time."

Metaphor: "It's a jungle out there."
Judgment: "This is completely unfair! You are more biased than I am."

We are each biased by the experiences we've had and the associations our minds have drawn from those experiences outside consciousness to guide that portion of our minds in selecting which habits we have built and use and those we haven't. When we recognize this type of experiential bias exists, we can rescue ourselves from periodic bouts of discomfort with other people by respecting their judgments as at least equally valid as ours.

By using this last category as a reminder to check if we have implied that our perspective is not just ours, but the "right" one, we can eliminate a majority of the opportunities in our interactions with other people to act stressed, indignant, shocked, angered, disappointed or burnt-out.

Judgmental implications can be made by something as simple as an inflection in our tone of voice. When we say, "Really?" and raise our tone at the end, have we just implied that we agree or not?

By familiarizing ourselves with our own tendencies to frequently imply judgments, we become much more sensitive to that practice when it comes back at us in conversation, in writing or over the airwaves.

It will be harder for us to be whipped into a frothy, emotional reaction by implicit appeals to judge other people, other classes of experience, even our own bodies and minds from experts and acquaintances alike. You will see and hear the news for what it is, competitive entertainers vying for your consuming dollar by appealing to your tendency to be drawn into judging the world along the lines those "impartial" talking heads suggest for you.

Ads for weight loss, hair replacement, automobiles and virtually everything else take on whole new dimensions for the informed consumer who pays attention to the biases being sold along with the products. Talk shows pit one group of prejudices against another, and hint which one is "right" so you will know which opinion to embrace. Simply noticing what gets on the air and what doesn't gives you a greater appreciation that attending to implied bias is a potent way to protect your mind from unwanted advertising.

The neurolinguistic programming experts used to say: "There is no right or wrong, there are only outcomes. If you don't like the outcomes you're getting, do something different." Of course we know there is a right and there is a wrong. The question the informed consumer asks is, "According to whom?"

In maneuvering these six categories of thinking habits and the one discipline for interrupting kinesthesia which drives them, there are a couple of guidelines which bear repeating.

Keep it simple and only practice one thing at a time. Spend a day, or even a week just exploring one area.

Use a video recorder and commercial TV. Rewinding is helpful.

Remember: after noticing, interrupting and saying your little piece (to yourself or out loud), get your attention out of your head and immediately into the world around you.

Finally, remember that habits are habits, and it takes time to build an onion. Enjoy the practice by making each effort a starting line and not a deadline.

o   o   o

Since meaning is subjective, implications are even more impactful on our habits than explanations. Usually they aren't challenged. All the exercises help you to practice guarding against unproductive implications and to minimize distracting internal dialogue.

8

My World Or Yours?

A n attorney who had attended my seminars called me one day and told me the following story:

"I was involved in a settlement negotiation for damages with the lawyer for the defendant. On behalf of my client, I started our talks with a request for a settlement of about $98,000. My opponent responded with a big zero. You might say we had some ground to cover.

"I decided to use what I had learned from your workshops about paying attention to nonverbal messages. I would make an offer and wait for my opponent to counter. When he said something like 'That's our final offer,' I'd just settle myself down and ask him if that was really all the money he was going to commit. If his body indicated 'No,' even if he said, 'Yes,' out loud, I would simply sit there and look at him.

"After several minutes, he'd break the silence and raise the offer. Then we'd go through the whole process again. At the end of our session we still hadn't settled. He had raised his offer to $60,000 and I'd come down to $92,000.

"As I looked through my calender to set an appointment for the following day, I told him we could get together at 10:30 for a few minutes since I had an eleven o'clock meeting scheduled.

"Watching my opponent carefully, I settled back in my chair and said casually, 'I wonder if I'll have to cancel that?'

"He replied that he didn't know why we're getting together at all. 'You've already got everything you're going to get,' he said. But his body conveyed a clear 'No.'

"Then I said, 'I think there's a middle ground between our two figures and I'm willing to bet we'll settle for $90,000.' He indicated yes, and said 'No.'

"I knew two things then. One: I could keep my eleven o'clock appointment, and two: I knew the amount of the final settlement offer."

My client let me know that he used this technique at every opportunity. It worked!

o   o   o

The anecdote the attorney related points out the reliability of information published in the *British Journal of Social and Clinical Psychology*. According to the article, only seven percent of all human communication is conducted by verbal content. The rest is carried on through tone of voice, the messages in the eyes and the movements of the body.

My client, the attorney, took advantage of those nonverbal signals in his settlement negotiations to create astonishing results. These are the same signals you receive when someone acts angry toward you, but is trying to hide it. That's what mixed messages are all about.

What mixed messages tell us is that the lips are saying one thing, but the body is saying something else. Everyone knows this from his own experience. My attorney friend knew that he could just sit and wait for his counterpart to raise his offer, because he'd practiced watching for those nonverbal signals without interference from his own. He trusted what he perceived his opponent's truer message to be. But what signs did he look for?

The answer to this question is the main concern of this chapter.

It is always helpful to remember that nobody but you has your mind. What is obvious to you with your history may be obscure or meaningless to the next person. What may be silly to you may be critically important to him, and vice versa. Most important, nobody talks himself into perceiving the world the way he does, so nobody's going to easily be talked *out* of a perception.

If you fail to communicate well with someone at the nonverbal level you've lost at least 93 percent of your connection with him. If you disagree on a word or phrase, but maintain the *non*verbal connection, you've only lost about 7 percent of the substance of the communication between you. The challenge comes in realizing and dealing with the fact that no two people respond in the same fashion to the same communication nonverbally any more than they respond the same to a spoken word like "power".

Go stand in front of the mirror or your video camera. Now, read the following lines out loud and watch and listen to yourself carefully. Make your delivery as straightforward as possible. Pretend you are addressing a group of professional peers:

"I have some pretty serious news to discuss. It is really a very serious situation we've got in front of us, and I want you all to have a chance to put in your two cents' worth about it."

Okay. If you wish to repeat your performance a second or third time until you're familiar with it, feel free. Again, if you have someone available to watch and listen to your performance with you, all the more helpful. But you can accomplish this all on your own.

Take a few moments now and with your eyes closed remember a time when you were not pleased, a time when you were acting very angry with the world or something in it. Note the sensations, the things you may have said to yourself, and bring back to the front of your mind the sights which faced you when you were experiencing that angry reaction. See, hear and even breathe that moment again, now.

When you're ready, address your group of peers again holding on to the anger you remember, and pretend you don't want them to know about it. Make sure you repeat your performance more than once and pay attention to your demeanor as you do so.

Okay. Take a couple of deep breaths and let them out slowly. Release that old angry memory. Now, please repeat the procedure of standing in front of the mirror two more times, only with these changes: the first time, remember a moment when you were feeling very strongly attracted to somebody in the room with you. The second time, recall a moment when you and somebody else in the room were cracking up about something nobody else was in on, and every time your eyes met, you would have to stifle another blast of snickers about the secret joke.

Hold each of those experiences in turn solidly in your head and read your announcement of "serious news" to your imaginary peers again. Do so as if you wished to avoid giving away your internal state of mind. Hold the old moment of attraction or mirth in the front of your mind, and speak as if you were trying to hide it from your audience. Repeat each a couple of times and pay attention.

The majority of you will have noticed several differences in your performances. If you didn't, run the exercise again and spend a bit more time reviving the past emotional reaction before reading your piece. If you still have trouble noticing the differences in your delivery, find yourself a live observer, and let him help you pick them out. They'll be there.

Everyone can stand some practice noticing that what goes on in his mind is inevitably reflected in his body and demeanor. Parents know that you cannot actually hide something from the kids; you can only obscure the details. The kids will know *something* is up, they just won't know exactly what it may be. The same is true for managers trying to hide some company secret from their peers and subordinates until the upper echelon gives them the "Okay" to spill the beans. By that time, everyone knew *something* was up; they just weren't sure what. Ditto in relationships, both casual and personal. Messages get across, even if they're mixed, unclear or deliberately hidden.

If you were lucky, you just had three opportunities to notice how, even in an artificial role-playing situation, the more you tried to hide a message, the more it leaked through in your demeanor. Some of you may have noticed differences in your voice's tone or volume. Some may have spoken louder or softer, faster or slower, depending on the hidden mind set. How many noticed a difference in your posture or your gestures? Did any of you catch a difference in facial expressions, head tilts and bobs, eye focus and movements?

Actions always have, and always will, speak louder than words. The challenge for the consumer learning to protect her own mind from the consequences of that fact comes in recognizing that her actions will not always convey the message she thinks they will.

There are people out there selling Active Ingredients in the field of nonverbal communication or "body language," too. That practice is not confined to verbal interchange. These "why" merchants will tell you that crossed arms on any individual, at any time she is listening to you, *means* always that she is not in agreement with you; that she is closed to your message. Common sense indicates the stupidity of that.

Quick, grab your Pez dispenser and come up with at least three equally plausible messages that crossed arms could be sending. How about a "too cold" room? What about sore shoulders? Or maybe a chair with no arms? Don't forget arms crossed beneath an unexpectedly broken bra strap.

During a recent election, I was featured several times on radio and in print media commenting on credibility and the candidates' nonverbal demeanor. Most interviewers expected me to mimic the common "wisdom" of individuals who sink thousands of dollars and hours into researching correlations between things like eye-blinks and "stress." Their simple, easy solution was that eye-blinks increase in frequency as the speaker's so-called stress level goes up.

You can invalidate all that research simply by remembering what it was like in early school days when you were in the middle of a tough test which you wished you'd been just a bit more prepared for, but which you were giving a strong effort to, nonetheless. Can you recall staring off into space toward the wall or out the window, desperately seeking an answer to a critically important question? Can you remember watching other kids sweat out the process the same way: eyes glazed and unblinking, seemingly for minutes at a time? Would you call that a *low*-stress situation?

What about another factor entirely overlooked by experiments already biased toward the Active Ingredient proposed in the experimentor's hypothesis? Stand in front of your mirror with a flashlight. Now give a little speech with it turned off, the first time. The second time, shine it right at your forehead as you talk. Count how many more times someone giving a speech on TV is likely to blink, before the "stress monster" ever even gets out of its limo in the parking lot.

What each interviewer discovered from talking with me is that the impact of any human communication lies not with the sender, but with the receiver! NLP used to use a phrase which I appreciate: The meaning of any communication is the response you get. Bear in mind that "response," just like all communication is at least 93 percent *non*verbal, and may have nothing to do with what the person says back to you. Think of a time when you were upset by some communication with somebody else, but used words in your response to try to hide that upset reaction. The meaning of his communication was your upset response, regardless of what he may have intended for it to be.

Go back over your four different speeches in the prior exercise. Take into account the differences in your demeanor as you shifted from one inner response to another. Imagine for a moment or two that an audience of fifteen different individuals, with fifteen different "ocean"-making minds were listening and attending fully to your performance. Can you begin to appreciate now that what you *intended* consciously to put across means next to nothing compared to how your performance was *taken* behind the eyes and ears of your beholders? Remember, nine times more of your message gets across without words and outside the reach of even the finest conscious intent.

What if your audience were a jury? What if that audience had been a committee you were trying to sell a hard-won proposal, a new contract, or a system for improving your children's education? What if it were the judge deciding your custody hearing? What if the audience was only one person: the most important person in your life? What if the angry reaction, the mirthful reaction or the lustful reaction was like most all of your habits —*outside* your conscious awareness? Are you sure you'd be communicating what you intended? How would you ever know? If you remain insensitive to the nonverbally advertised responses of other people to your attempts to reach them, you will never be able to know how well, or poorly, your message has been received. It is strictly how a message is received that makes all the difference. You can have the purest intentions in the world and still convey the opposite of what you mean. And that will be conveyed nine times more than the *spoken* part of your message.

Most distressing of all is the fact that your attempts to later talk somebody out of an erroneous impression she formed from your all your communication, not just the words, will almost always make matters even more uncomfortable. Creatures of habit do not talk themselves into their reactions, nor are they very easily talked out of them. Give yourself five good reasons not to feel strongly about your best friend, if you want an example.

Before we get into more specific aspects of the nonverbal etiquette which this section offers you to begin practicing, let's go over a few general rules for nonverbal messages which respect the receiver of communication as well as the sender. They apply in all situations where humans are interacting.

If you are communicating with one person at the outset, take some time to notice how he uses his body to express himself. (If this is a phone conversation, the following distinctions still apply, but only at the level of noises, not gestures.) As you first approach him, or are approached, shut down as much of your regular walking-around behavior as you comfortably can to give the individual a chance to advertise what is "normal" for him in this situation. Sighing will help you interrupt a behavioral habit (as well as thinking habits) outside consciousness.

Notice in his performance the very same things you noticed in yours in the mirror a little while back. Look at how close he stands to you, how rapidly he speaks, how little or large his gestures are and what the rhythms, tones, volumes and spaces in his speech are like. As you learned from your own exercise, the "package" that carries even two or three lines gives away a tremendous amount of a "this is the way I've always done things" habit.

Once you've noticed a few distinctions like pace, proximity and amplitude in gestures, do what any polite person would do: respond in kind. Avoid just slavishly mimicking everything she does, and how she does it. That is not polite: that's obnoxious. But be certain that if you are in the company of a fast-talking, arm-waving, eyebrow-wiggling person who stands and leans way back from you to talk that you avoid responding with an even, soft, regular voice, while seated leaning very close to her face. That isn't responding in kind to her: it's probably responding with your own reaction to her.

Think of communication with other people as travelling to a foreign country whose language you do not speak. You are aware that native speakers usually will respond much more productively to someone who at least makes the effort—no matter how awkward—to use a few words of the language of the country she is visiting, rather than simply speaking English loudly and slowly.

Incidentally, anytime you hear someone cry, "No, no, no...you don't understand what I mean!" you've just observed someone loudly speaking *his* version of English to a mind foreign to him, then acting upset when the stranger proves not to have the same brain as the "misunderstood" person. First, he expects the other to "know what he means," and then he conveys a criticism for not holding the same associations in mind as the speaker's.

In my book, that's two hurts for the price of none. The response of the listener is the meaning of your communication; if you perceive him as "not understanding" you, it is your responsibility to alter your approach to meet *his* model of the world rather than berating him for not having your brain and your vocabulary with its associations which are highly-prized only by you.

In meetings, you will still be communicating usually to only one person at a time, so the general rule of responding in kind to one person's habits still holds. Presentations to groups are another story which will be covered later, but you can still start well with a group if you get there early enough to at least demonstrate some respectful responses to individuals before the formal talking begins.

Remember, all our emotional, mental and behavioral habits are cued outside consciousness by the Engine of sensation. One of the most common, and direct, cues to *have* that sensation is your response to another person. And the vast majority of our responses - both comfortable and otherwise - are generated by the package your words come in: your demeanor. In less than fifteen seconds, with most people in most situations, simply responding in kind to their general habits of putting themselves across in the world will prompt a comfortable reaction to you outside their conscious notice. That's not everything, but it's sure a nice place to start.

Next, keep very clear on the fact that there is no objective reality when it comes to the human mind. What's obvious to you isn't so obvious to other people. If you go back over the six categories of implicit messages from Chapter VII, you'll recall a few of the many biased reactions awaiting you in the minds of people who are attending to your demeanor. Your best chance to catch up to the process a little lies in keeping as much of your attention near the present moment as possible.

So, build an onion (train car) for sighing as you begin each important remark or question. You needn't make your sighing so demonstrative that other people are distracted by it; you can do it in complete silence. The pause you create will also help them pull their attention our of their Caboose, and back into their portion of the conversation, thus helping avoid some of the more bizarre reactions they could otherwise have.

Be certain, to the very limit of your capacities, to practice *avoiding* the exercise we started this chapter practicing. Remember the difference between delivering a message **In your Body** or **In your Head**. If you are discussing a person with whom you were angered with a third party, be very careful to interrupt your Train of Thought as you begin, to avoid habitually replaying all the behavioral references which indicate that you have "boiling blood." Likewise, if you are quoting a conversation verbatim to a third party later and you replay an insult that was spoken to someone else, be sure you turn slightly away from your listener's face as you repeat that insult out loud.

That primate across from you is very sensitive to the package your words arrive in. If you act out the lustful, or angry, or disdainful, or worshipful behaviors you've used with someone *else*, as you are facing this one, don't be too surprised if you have trouble getting things across well to her. Nine times more of your message is mixed-up with situations which are only happening in your head. Your listener will be distracted at least, if not completely thrown off, by the mismatch in your actions and words.

Likewise, for quoting old conversations to someone else, face-to-face. If your quotations come complete with your old demeanor intact, and you fail to shift your gaze slightly from her face as you replay the comments you originally gave to somebody else, this person's mind will have no choice but to react as if the message were somehow meant for her—even if she consciously knows that isn't the case.

My old friend Paul, of the "heads will roll" story, was once on-stage with me presenting to a group of people interested in improved performance. When we got off, he stopped me and threatened to end my life if I ever "lost quotes on him" again the way I had just then. I quickly reviewed my performance and picked out exactly what had prompted his response.

I had several times repeated things which other experts had said. Many of these quotes were highly critical. Every one of them had been delivered as I looked directly at Paul. Imagine me gesturing and looking at Paul, saying, "Descartes says, 'This is obviously stupid!'" And, even more distressing, I was fully animated, acting out the critiques as well as mouthing them. Most disturbing of all was that the audience was paying attention and forming associations for that communication, regardless of how poorly sorted out it had been.

If you repeat an insult someone gave you to a third person's face, and you fail to avoid acting out your insulted response and steer the focus slightly away from the listener's face, most of your communication will embody that old insult. Only now it will be you sending the insult, and your listener receiving it. Any old response you don't wish to communicate to your listener(s) would be most comfortably delivered by getting your attention onto the behavior of your listeners and off the old response, so you avoid acting it out yet again.

Think how many times you've witnessed someone acting

out an angry reaction toward someone in his life, while asking for advice from his listener, only to find the listener picking up the angry reaction as displayed and feeding the fire instead of helping put it out.

Finally, if you are planning to help guide other people's performance as a parent, a teacher, a trainer or a manager, it can be very helpful to remember that human reactions are based mainly upon behavior and not on intentions or words. Keep the expression of verbal "understanding" in its proper place. Remember that each mind has a different set of meanings stored in it, and your job is more to guide *actions*, not speech.

The example of the typical sales team meeting is useful in practicing putting first things first in communication.

Imagine the team leader, the boss, standing at the white board in front of a roomful of her regional sales or marketing team. They have just received word from on high in the company that their recent performance is "not good enough" and they must improve. The boss writes down the deadline: "3% real increase in actual revenues generated by the end of next quarter".

Automatically, everyone in the room does a calculation in his or her head. Each one comes up with a number which indicates a 3% increase in business he or she generated last quarter. Meanwhile, the boss is writing the team's total and new goal on the board. Some of the listeners have, by then, also figured out how big of an increase in business they need to generate for each of the next 90 days, on average, to meet their individual part of that goal.

Here's where the fun begins. The boss starts requesting input. The boss wants everybody to help make a list of all the reasons why they've had trouble so far. They all eventually shout out a bunch of plausible Pez-like reasons which they all pretend were visible to them hiding inside the minds of their customers—

even though those people are not even in the room!

Then, having elicited all the alleged blocks to improvement, the boss erases that board and begins asking for suggestions for ways to break through those blocks to progress, "now that we know what we're up against." Slowly, people offer suggestions for things each person believes could be done differently, or new things to do, to help out. They all are offering labels for whole complexes of associated habits in their own individual minds.

Here is the chance for the boss to act respectfully towards the differences among the minds in the team. Rather than the standard approach, which entails "prioritizing" all the suggestions (which mean something different to each brain in the room), and then voting on some arbitrary number of them, like five, for everyone to then "go out and implement, or heads will roll," what if the boss did something unexpected?

What if the boss made sure that each salesperson or marketer had contributed at least one suggestion for how to increase his numbers, and had written it down? What if the boss then said, "Everybody copy this list, but don't worry. We'll have a typed copy forwarded to you, also. Now, I know that each of you knows your customers and clients more than the rest of us do. I also know that we all are aware there's a difference between theory and practice. So, I want you to pick from this list the approaches *you* believe will help you serve your particular people most effectively. But I don't want you to stop there."

"Two weeks from now, I'd like each of you to submit something else you had a chance to try, or maybe were forced to try on-the-spot, by the real-world situation with one of your people. I'll collect those suggestions and pass them out to everybody here. This list here is a good start, but we all know it's different when you take it off the paper and put it in practice. Rather than limiting ourselves, or waiting till it's too late, I want to rely on your abilities, your creativity and your knowledge of your own people to get this team moving. Any questions?"

So, when you go out to practice:

First sigh, settle your regular package of reactions down long enough to respond in kind to the general demeanor of other people. Avoid slavish mimicry.

Second, keep your attention on the people in front of you. Notice if you've slipped into displaying behavior that has nothing to do with them, and a lot to do with your personal history. Stop, sigh, and start over when you catch yourself modeling responses which belong to people other than the one you're talking with.

Third, keep first things first. When you are attempting to guide other people's reactions and performances, remember that the mind responds well to direction (actions) and very poorly to dictation (words). Build a habit for keeping the two in their respective places.

Any questions?

o   o   o

It's not what you say, but how you say it that makes a mark on people. People form a feeling-impression from your demeanor. These feelings are non-specific, but once impressions are formed as feelings, it is almost impossible to take them back.

*"Everybody experiences
far more than he understands.
Yet it is experience,
rather than understanding,
which influences behavior.*

Marshall McLuhan

9

Mirror, Mirror

Nonverbal communication simply means conveying a message without words. There are dozens of programs on the market which purport to help people recognize what is being communicated to them in body language. The reader would be wise to disregard programs which simply translate specific gestures into specific Active Ingredients or emotions. The idea in this chapter is to help you to improve communication with other people by learning to appreciate and respond to their personal signals.

Let's start with an exercise of a different nature. When you have read the instructions, please take the time to make the suggested observations before you read on. It will give the rest of this material, as well as the following chapters, a higher degree of validity.

Visit a mall, airport or any place where there is a lot of people traffic. Look at parents interacting with their children.

Observe couples. Notice how the messages people are sending come across through their movements, postures and gestures. Visit several popular restaurants and bars. Watch until you see an unaccompanied individual attach himself to another person. Observe what happens to the behavioral "signatures" of the two after they have been sitting together for a while. If the mall you've chosen has a theater, look at the people standing in line. See if you can pick out who is in whose company by the demeanor each person demonstrates.

Were you able to confirm that when it comes to human communication at the nonverbal level, it is still "monkey see, monkey do?" Did you notice children walking just like their parents? Did you catch couples mimicking each other's gestures, postures and movements? Did you take note of when each of a newly-introduced pair in the bar began matching some of the behavioral output of the other? Did you notice what happened if this matching did *not* occur?

How about the line in front of the movie house? How far away can you be and still discern with accuracy who is in line with whom, even if he or she is not standing next to one another?

Did you observe people stop conversing in order to raise a glass in unison? Did you notice people leaning in or out of conversations virtually in tandem? How many heads tilted in similar directions? How many nods, finger-pointings, sighs, shoulder dips, leg crossings and facial movements were mirrored?

If you have not noticed any of this behavior, go back and look again. Now that you know what you're looking for you'll wonder how you could have missed it the first time.

Much has been written and taught about the phenomenon of mirroring. Whole schools of psychology have used mirroring as a treatment method. Later, that same approach was translated into a million-selling "quickie" management tome. As children, we all play at mirroring.

Without taking too much meaning from the fact that most primates who are getting along in their groups will match each other's postures and behavior, I can safely state that it is noticeable. You just proved that. And it is a fact that it is not a conscious phenomenon the majority of time. Of all the people you observed, you were most assuredly the only one who was conscious of matching behavior on display.

Dr. Dave Dobson commented on two primates mirroring each other's general demeanor as the clue that neither animal perceived a threat present in the other. As you may have noticed when two human animals are acting upset, mirroring is usually put on hold.

Mirroring or matching behavior occurs naturally. You did not have to pay the people at the mall to perform for you. And by observation alone you can confirm that this natural behavior exists more frequently between two people who do not feel threatened, than between people who are in an uncomfortable situation.

As you apply mirroring or matching in a simple, directed fashion, you will discover that people react as if you had acknowledged them on a more fundamental level than a verbal greeting can convey. This theory is easily tested by anyone who has ever gone into her office and noticed that people, on the phone and face-to-face, tend to speak their "hellos" or their "good mornings" exactly in the same way to everyone they greet. If called upon to repeat what they say to the people they habitually greet every day, most of them would be hard-pressed to come up with the words they had used. *We are all creatures of habit.*

The first gathering of trial lawyers I ever worked with was a hand-picked group selected by the president, John Carey, of the state's trial lawyers association. My experiences in mirroring had a great deal to do with my getting the training contract with that group.

John, the president, had been introduced to the conscious application of mirroring in a nonverbal communication course just before meeting me. Shortly thereafter, he had to take a deposition from an expert witness. Being a plaintiff's attorney, he frequently took medical testimony from experts hired by the defending company or insurance provider. Many times the defendants ended up using the same experts in a variety of different cases, due to the lack of professionals willing to spend a major portion of their time in the courts instead of tending to their practices.

During our session on mirroring, John mentioned a doctor's name whereupon several of the attorneys in the room groaned out loud. They had had similar experiences with the gentleman in question. This particular expert witness was prone to giving the briefest depositions on record. He answered questions in monosyllables, was never forthcoming and acted routinely disdainful of the proceedings. John decided this would be a valuable test for the practice of mirroring.

Imagine his surprise, and that of the other lawyers, when the good doctor, whom John mirrored constantly throughout the deposition, actually began answering the questions in complete sentences. The man ended up offering John information he had not asked for, and seemed to enjoy the longest deposition he had ever delivered. John commented that the opposing counsel actually had to stop the good doctor on a couple of occasions from speaking too much on certain key subjects.

When approached with respect, *both* verbally and nonverbally, people are more likely to respond in a productive manner. This was the case with the doctor. John addressed him with respect and the man responded expansively. Since interactions among people are the final arbiters of our failures and success-es, we must be aware of how potent carefully directed mirror-ing is.

From the lady who overcame seven years of discomfort and the brick-wall-type behavior of her father and owner of the fam-ily business, to the therapist whose patient rose above a major physical difficulty, to an attorney getting a ruling from a judge without speaking *one word* out loud, we learn to pay heed to the phenomenon of mirroring. We don't need a "technique." We might do well to just *pay attention.*

I continue to hear success stories from my clients who tes-tify to the benefits—professionally and personally—of using mirroring to communicate outside consciousness.

It doesn't even have to be a face-to-face encounter with peo-ple in order to be able to match their responses. The following is a good example:

I know of an organization which did a great deal of its busi-ness through telephone selling. Most of the company's prospec-tive customer contacts were initiated by outside activities. When these prospects called in to the company, the calls were handled by a bank of receptionists and handed on to salespeople who fol-lowed up the leads. By simply training the receptionists to match the tone quality, pace and volume of the caller's voice, the com-pany tripled favorable responses to the incoming calls which resulted in increased sales .

The most important part of learning to mirror constructive-ly is to know when to quit. Those of you who grew up with younger brothers or sisters can attest to the fact that the most annoying deed a sibling can do is to mimic every single thing you do or say. Triumph in this torturous game came when the mimicked siblings could no longer stand their shadow, stomped their feet and shouted, "Stop that!" In reply the tormenting child would smile devilishly, stomp his foot and shout, "Stop that!" right back.

Since being sensitive to mimicking doesn't diminish as we grow older, we learn to distract ourselves with "more important" things. We have to ignore the sensation along our midline which is generated by our mind in order to get our attention.

In the alternative, we could come up with a productive version of that sensation for anyone we meet, simply by greeting that person verbally and nonverbally, utilizing mirroring. That, of course, would require a bit more attention on someone *other* than ourselves.

That sensation is the engine which draws out people's mental, emotional and behavioral habits. We can profit by inviting them to steer that engine of sensation in a more beneficial direction.

Mirroring is a simple process. First notice that *something* in a person's demeanor of which he is not conscious—like head tilts, posture, tone of voice gestures or a dozen other characteristics. How a person walks, how he uses his voice, how he sits in his chair all are important to match because these functions are fundamental as well as habitual, and therefore unlikely to be consciously noticed when matched.

You do not have to match everything a person does, just one or two things. Nor do you have to match them for very long which may be contrary to what some of you may have learned from other sources. The length of time required to match someone is determined by his responses, as in any greeting, but it usually is less than twenty seconds.

Once you have determined what behavior to match, replay it to the other party. It need not be a perfect match. If the other person crosses his legs at the knee, crossing yours at the ankle will usually do it. If his hands are in his pockets, yours can be clasped behind you which achieves the desired result. If her head tips to the left, tipping yours to the right will do as well as tipping it to the left.

Once you begin consciously matching people, one of the first things you will notice is how often both parties are already mirroring each other *outside* consciousness. That simply serves to remind you that any two primates, even chimpanzees, will mimic one another. The following steps will separate you from the chimps.

You know that matching gets their attention. If you have practiced the suggestions from the last chapter, you may have discovered people are acting more attentively as soon as you adopt some of their general behaviors. In moving up to the step of actually greeting them outside consciousness—and getting a response outside consciousness—you can measure *how* they show that increased level of attentiveness. Here's how:

Notice and match something in someone's demeanor. Then, pay close attention to how he indicates that he has noticed you, outside his conscious awareness. Is it more direct eye contact, or did the corners of his mouth turn up slightly? Those are two of the most common responses to mirroring to look for. Slight nods, head tilts or straightening up just after being matched are others. Avoid restricting your attention to the head and face of the other person. Some people move a hand or a foot when responding to your matching. Some folks frown, a few turn their heads away. Some people lean forward or backwards. There are hundreds of more individualized responses which are too varied to mention. Just match the gestures and pay immediate attention to the results. The mind outside consciousness works very quickly. The you've-got-more-of-my-attention response won't be long in coming.

The final step of this nonverbal greeting is the most important. When you notice how a person responds to your initial mirroring, no matter what form that response takes, feed it back. When you see or hear how the individual reacts to your mirroring something in his demeanor, match that bit of behavior. Feed it right back to him, exactly the way he does it.

That person's mind selected that behavior from all those at his disposal to register his attention to your mirroring. Your mirroring is not consciously noticed, and the bit of behavior selected to acknowledge your mirroring is not consciously selected, either. You will be the only one conscious of the exchange. At that moment, you have a chance to confirm with him that the message he just sent was in response to your effort. Feed back to that person, as precisely as you can, what he did to acknowledge your matching.

Precision is a little more important in this case. If the corners of his mouth go up slightly and you grin back broadly, you have not done well. If he raised his head slightly, then lowered it back to its original position and you feed back vigorous nodding, that is not feedback. If he focuses more directly on your eyes, and you stare him down intensely with the whites of your eyes showing, then you've blown it.

That person has rehearsed for a lifetime how to advertise that his attention has just been captured by the primate in front of him.

Respect those years of rehearsal outside consciousness by watching the response and feeding it back as precisely as you can. The exception to this rule is that you want to avoid overdoing mirroring, so that your efforts become obvious.

Incidentally, outside of situations where I have been training people to scrutinize mirroring behavior, I have rarely had anyone over the age of seven take conscious notice of my mirroring. If that happens to you, and the person asks you if you are mimicking or mocking her, avoid lying.

Simply say something like, "What do you know about that—we *are* standing alike." Just leave out the part about you doing it on purpose, and shift to something less obvious to mirror and start over.

Expect small children to respond *and* notice you consciously. They have not yet learned that the allegedly valuable parts of the world are in their caboose of spoken interpretations and solutions. They are still busy actually watching the people around them. If you match them, they'll most likely laugh and give you something else to match.

When you match a bit of behavior with anyone, notice the response of increased attention, and when you feed back that response one of two things will happen. Either the person's mind will somehow amplify that response, or nothing happens. If nothing happens, you have not completed your greeting outside consciousness, and you may wish to start again. If, on the other hand, the person amplifies the response she showed to your initial matching, then you've gotten a message back from her mind outside consciousness that indeed she is attending specifically to you.

Notice that the behavior you fed back was selected *outside consciousness* to respond to your mirroring which was also outside conscious notice. If you feed back the behavior the person uses to advertise increased attention and it is amplified in response, you've used *his* other than conscious responses to confirm *his* other than conscious attention. If his mind alters the reaction you have matched, then you have stepped beyond "monkey see, monkey do!"

In review, greeting a person nonverbally and confirming her attention outside consciousness is a three step process:

1. Notice and mirror some bit of behavior.

2. Notice and feed back the response.

3. Watch and listen for amplification.

That's all the mirroring you need to do in order to set up effective communication outside consciousness. You will wish to maintain the general demeanor of the person you communicate with by responding in kind to him, but your mirroring will take no more than thirty seconds at the outset of any communication.

I strongly suggest you practice mirroring a lot. Creatures of habit do not simply install a new habit of action by deciding to do so. It requires some rehearsing. If you want this communication skill to be available, practice it in everyday situations.

A good example of amplification is the following: If you receive a smile in response to your initial matching, and you feed back that smile precisely, that smile will broaden. Sometimes, amplification turns the smile the other way. Sometimes a head tilt, if amplified, becomes a head straightening. Instead of leaning further one way, the amplification turns out to be a lean in the other direction. As long as the alteration occurs with the same behavior used to recognize your initial matching—and not some new and different demeanor—that qualifies as amplification. .

Some caution: About one or two out of twenty people will simply break off contact with you when you attempt to mirror them. Avoid being a mind reader and interpret that behavior as an insult. You have accomplished getting their attention. If you feed back their "break-off" response, about half of them will respond after all.

In our society of unprotected minds and increasing alienation, a few people are so unaccustomed to the conscious expression of that midline sensation, that they are unprepared to continue traveling down the track which requires them to actually consciously experience a feeling.

The alternate reaction also occurs frequently: Someone may

respond to your three-step greeting by launching into her life story. So few people are conscious of the sense of connection that when it happens to them they go overboard.

Be polite and listen to as much as you are able. Then, if you wish to curtail a person's flow of words, mismatch her, feeding back the opposite message of her behavior, and you will have to race her to stop the conversation.

One of the nicest things about familiarizing yourself with this beginning version of communication outside consciousness is that you can choose *not to* mirror someone. You will have validated this approach's efficacy in garnering almost anyone's full attention rapidly after just a day or two of practice. One thing you will inevitably notice is how much mirroring and responding is going on around you. It has been going on all your life. Only most of us have bought labels for it like: kismet, natural sales ability, love (or lust) at first sight, sensitivity, understanding, and so forth. The mind is always attentive and always working. If you point your conscious attention toward someone and keep it there, you are very likely to end up mirroring him— sometimes even in a threatening situation.

There are times in which it helps to minimize the amount of attention you are drawing from an individual—especially if your personal safety is at stake. Staring at a potentially dangerous person could lead to mirroring, capture attention and trigger undesired results. By becoming sensitive to mirroring, you can elect *not* use the technique. You can avoid inviting someone to attend to you with the part of his mind which cues his habits of action and thinking. You simply remain faceless by using your mind's talents to protect yourself.

Finally, as you practice, you will find a few people who will simply not respond, no matter how long you match them. These people are so busy reacting to old images, voices and sensations in their heads that they can't center their attention on your efforts. They are giving you and your mind the message, advertised with *93 percent* of their communication that nothing you have to offer is as important to them as their own head. These people are often the ones who wonder why they have so few friends, so little trustworthy help at work, and such unsatisfying relationships in general.

The next time someone calls your name and you jerk your head around and respond with something like, "Huh?" you'll know you have been doing it too. However, *now* you can pick up where you left off. When a person pops into your conscious awareness, be aware that it is a signal to greet all parts of his mind.

o   o   o

Mirroring does not *lead* the person being imitated; rather it is directed courtesy. Greeting nonverbally is nine times more important than verbally.

10

See Me, Hear Me, Feel Me

During a conversation I had with Dr. Lawrence LeShan, a well-respected, no-nonsense practitioner of psychology, several people present asked his opinion on the latest techniques, scientific discoveries and approaches being used in therapy. He replied: "I consider anything that has not been around for at least twenty years a fad. I don't pay any attention to fads."

This chapter offers the next step in communication outside consciousness. The material presented here stems from from my experience with neurolinguistic programming (NLP). Since Doctor John Grinder and Richard Bandler began their work in NLP in the early seventies, I believe this approach passes Dr. LeShan's fad test. The basic awarenesses I gleaned from NLP are well acknowledged in scientific circles and are being utilized in numerous fields from education to neuroscience.

This exercise requires paper, pen and your VCR. Record several spontaneous reaction shows—talk shows, panel discussions, news programs, or anything which features several people on camera who are not reading from a telepromter or using memorized dialogue. Review what you have taped, and select a few close-ups of a person speaking for at least twenty or thirty seconds. Also locate some views which show the person from the waist up or preferably at full length. Draw a big circle on your paper to represent a face. Put in the eyes. Draw a line horizontally through the eyes, across the whole page. Up and to the right of the face, and the same on the left, mark the letter "S." Mark an "S" down and to the right of the face, and another down and to the left. Finally, at either end of the horizontal line passing through the eyes, mark an "S".

Now, go back and print in tiny letters the word "Sight" for the two "Ss" on top, the word "Sound" for the two "Ss" across the middle line (even with the eyes), the word "Sound" for the "S" on the bottom right side of the diagram and the word "Sensation" for the "S" on the bottom left.

Take your diagram to the television set and watch one of the close-ups you taped with the sound turned down. Carefully watch the person's eye movements as he talks. Make a little mark near each "S" as his eyes move left or right as he talks. Feel free to use the pause button and rewind the tape as many times as necessary.

When you see the person's eyes drift down and to *his* left, mark that as a down-left motion on your chart, even though as you face him his eyes are pointing to *your* right. In communication it is the response, not your intention, which makes the difference. Use *his* reference for left and right, not your own. Down and to his right is "sensation."

Just as with noticing people's natural tendency to mirror the actions of others, you may be surprised to see that their eyes actually point as the diagram demonstrates quite frequently while they are communicating. This, too, has been going on around you all your life. You have noticed and responded to it outside consciousness. On occasion, this factor alone may have determined the quality of your life at that time. It is important to act on this level of communication *inside* your conscious awareness.

If you recall the "ocean" exercise, you'll remember that all the experiences which are stored, associated and referenced by your habits of thinking, are composed of sensory-based information. Everything in your mind is constructed from a combination of sights, sounds and sensations. That means that a large portion of your thinking habits outside consciousness happen to be words or sounds, but many of these stored associations are also sensations and sights.

Demonstrate this for yourself: Think of something important. Now, think of something dull. Next, think of anything at all. Were any of the experiences you recalled *not* composed of a collection of sights, sounds and sensations? Find something in your head which isn't! Sensory perceptions are the basic building blocks for the experiences which are later associated and reinforced, like building an onion, into habits of thought and action: the cars on your train.

Every experience is stored with all its sensory data intact. But your mind doesn't always select all those bits of experience when it pops something into consciousness. Nor does your mind use every portion of each experience stored to formulate your habits. The cars on your train of thought are composed of reactions which are primarily built from just one of the three aspects of sensory experience—either sights, sounds or feelings.

Some of us remember our grandmother's voice as clearly as if she were in the room. Others find it easier to picture Granny, but have a hard time hearing her. Some can do both with ease;

some of us have a sense of what it felt (or feels) to be in her company.

Our mind in consciousness is relegated to only seven bits of information per second to compose each conscious thought. These seven bits typically favor one of the sensory systems over the other two. This fact has led to a great misunderstanding among people who have studied various methods of communicating through the advertising of these sensory systems. Because we each tend to express more of one sense area than the other two in our demeanor, some people have drawn the conclusion that this sensory bias exists to the same extent outside consciousness—in the mind at large.

It does not.

Our brain has a visual cortex located toward the rear of our heads. Jokes about "eyes in the back" are actually based in fact. A part of our brain called the Site of Broca sorts out and makes "sense" of all the noises our ears collect and our mind recalls—all day long. Our brain has various voluntary and autonomic tools, including our spinal column and the limbic system to indulge the sensation side of life. Nobody is missing any of this equipment. Few have any damage to it. But, most of us habitually utilize one of those three systems over the others to "make sense" of our worlds on a day-to-day basis.

Since the mind, the brain and the body are interconnected, it will come as no surprise to you to discover that we advertise more in our demeanor than just how we have noticed we can match and be matched by other primates. We also have some ways of letting those who pay attention to us know exactly which sensory systems we are expressing ourselves with, and, therefore, are sensitive to at any given moment.

The primary way this advertising happens is through eye movements. Someone long ago said that the eyes are the window of the soul. You can prove for yourself that they are at least the window to the mind.

Review the charts and observe that each person had a majority of eye movements concentrated in one system over the others. Notice that while the actions of the first person may have required you to go back over the tape several times to get a count accumulated, you quickly became aware of these motions more easily. You have practiced noticing and reacting to these signals all your life without knowing it. It will take no more than a few weeks of paying conscious attention to them to build a habit for recognizing them and what they reveal.

The next step in practicing will be to return to the mall, or anywhere people gather in numbers, to observe eye movements both close up and from a distance.

o   o   o

Our habits of action reveal through gestures and sensory-biased phrases which sensory system is in play in our mind as we express that mind at every moment.

The phrases are the simplest:

I see you are making a point. You have shown us all before. It seemed like a bright idea at the time it first appeared, but I see the big picture even sharper now. Let's put it in a framework we can all look at the same way ... Or,

You have said the same thing before, although when I heard it the first time, I'm not sure it rang as true to me then as hearing it now. I believe something has clicked for me, and what I might do now is put your comments in a language we all can listen to together, now ... Or,

I remember feeling really nice about your proposal when you last brought it up. It grabbed me then, but I clearly feel its impact more fully now. I think all that remains is for me to put it into a form we can all handle, so we can run with it.

Same message, three different sensory "flavors". First sight, then sound, and finally feeling. Notice that there are words, like "clear" which cross easily from one system to the other. A person presently biased toward sounds "hears clearly," while another sees just as "clearly." There is a huge vocabulary of sensory-biased terms.

Please begin your search for them now. Turn down the brightness on those tapes, and find out for yourself if people really use more of one type of sense-words than others. When you have demonstrated that to your satisfaction, listen more closely to your phone conversations, your idle chatter and your serious discussions. You will be surprised.

The third and last indicator of sensory bias in communication comes across in certain gestures. Let's start with crossed arms. No gesture translates directly to a word like disagreement, nor to an emotional reaction like hostility. Nonverbal means no words. But crossed arms do most certainly indicate that a certain portion of the mind's attention is momentarily biased toward one sensory system over the other. That system is the auditory one. Crossed arms indicate that someone is committing a good portion of his attention at the moment to noises, or talking—in their head. That habit of thinking is revealed by an equally habitual gesture.

If you look back at some of the conclusions people draw from this "I'm-talking-to-myself" behavioral signal, they begin to make sense. Someone who fails to respect the fact that by crossing my arms I have just signalled, "I am presently *less* available to hear what someone may be saying, as I am indulging my hearing *inside* my head," may incorrectly interpret my "I'm-talking-in-here" signal to mean "I disagree." But, just because people have been rude, and have not let Mr. Arms-crossed finish, and *then* say their piece when they *manage to get* his attention is no reason to condemn him. After all, he demonstrated by his crossed arms that he was busy in there. They just failed to "listen" to his gesture.

Other gestures indicating attention to the auditory, or sound portion of the mind's activities are: rhythmic motions in the extremities, or in whole body movements—like nodding or swaying; hands held over the ears or to the mouth in "telephone" positions; and verbatim note-taking. Reading, writing and detailed outlining, charting and even graphing indicate a preference for the auditory side of life.

Gestures associated with visual bias are: palms-down, pointing and framing; vague sweeping gestures indicating an expanse seen only in the mind's eye; staring at people, objects and vistas which nobody else present can see.

Finally, gestures involving bias toward sensation, or kinesthesia, include: arhythmic motions and facial grimaces; touching, rubbing and exploring parts of the body; hands planted along the midline of the body from the bridge of the nose to the lower abdomen; vigorously punctuated gestures; palms up and pantomiming actions to get the message across.

Again, review your tapes and look at the waist-up or full-length versions for these gestures. By now, you probably won't be quite so surprised, except perhaps to find out just how much you've been reacting without paying attention at all to it.

You are now familiar with the fact that everything you have in the available portions of your mind is constructed from the sensory bits of experience, associated into patterns, and expressed as habits in action and thought. What you may not have consciously realized until this moment is that we all advertise our sensory preferences in every single interaction—face-to-face, and even on the phone.

Not only do we advertise our preferences, but we respond to that advertising as well. Where do you think all these gut feelings and intuitions you had about people have come from all your life? What prompted those moments of instant attraction or dislike? They all stem from uninformed, but potent advertising.

Here is perhaps the most valuable observation in this book: *We are not born expressing a preference for one system over the other in our habits of response.*

We *learn* to develop a bias toward one flavor over the others. But we can learn to balance them. And, considering that the world sends you a variety of twenty thousand bits of sensory information every second, it may be an advisable course.

It is essential to learn balance if you are looking for a greater measure of success dealing with others. There is no guarantee that another person will see eye-to-eye with us; speak the same language; or feel the way we do about things, unless you make sure you are using the 93 percent of your communication which encompasses those favorite flavors to get your messages *clearly* across to them—their way.

In his wonderful book *Mastery,* George Leonard points out that people who go into an activity which requires practice to develop skill, do so in only a few ways. These approaches break down into two categories: the people who want to get to the goal, or master the skill, and those who just practice, for the sake of practicing. The latter, he points out, are the *only* ones who ever achieve mastery.

If you indeed have read this book from the beginning, you will have observed that when it comes to figuring out human relations, there just are no simple, easy solutions. Each of the exercises and activities for you to practice is designed to bring you closer to achieving effective human relations. The exercises have no deadline, no end-point; they are starting lines for you. They have the added advantage of working very well.

Here are some suggestions on how to encourage and rebuild the balanced use of all three sensory preferences in your head. You may not make it all the way—but then neither have I, so far. However, even travelling a few miles down those still unfamiliar tracks promises astonishing benefits for your mind, just like the stories about those who have gone before you have indicated.

If you wish to be inoculated against our cultural habit of the *Active Ingredient*, then you will eventually be forced to make a choice: Are you going to seek your success in life by improving your abilities for interacting with others, or are you going to sharpen your ability to deal with the world from your personal perspective before all else? Are you going to act as if we cannot control the process of human interaction and predict the end results, or act as if everybody, everywhere, owns your brain?

NLP materials regarding sight, sound and sensation—in much different form than presented here—are among the current popular crop of tapes and seminar presentations handled by the two largest business-training companies in this country, through the efforts of my colleague, Charles Faulkner. This information is available to and valued by many people in all walks of life. Use my version of NLP as it most benefits you.

When you observe taped and live subjects for these exercises, you may have discovered that people tend to scramble rather than clearly express the indicators of these sensory systems: eye movements, phrases and gestures. All you need to do is find an accommodation between two out of three of the indicators. To make things even easier, one of the accommodations is almost always the eyes.

One more time—return to your tapes and charts. Replay the

sections where you already know that the majority of eye movements lean in the direction of either sights, sounds or sensations. Find out whether the person's gestures or the sensory-biased phrases he uses lean more towards the system indicated by the eyes. In the majority of cases, you'll see a clear preference. Occasionally, there will be a preponderance of gestures and phrases heading down a different track than the eye movements do. This is fairly rare, but it happens. If it is consistent, then act as if the two-out-of-three rule applies, even though the eyes point you elsewhere.

Practice responding to people at this next higher step of communication in small bites. Spend a day or two attending to just visual eye movements in your communications and respond to them in kind. Get used to communicating and just talking at the same level *inside* conscious awareness. Spend just as many days acknowledging and sending back both auditory and feeling eye movements. Be careful that you are actually following the movements of the person's eyes and not his head. Some people lean their head down and right, for example, while running their eyes up, not down at all.

Then, do the same with gestures and phrases. Remember this is a step beyond mirroring. That is the equivalent of a nonverbal greeting. This entails meeting that person at the level at which she is constructing experiences to respond to the world. If she uses one sound-type gesture, like twirling a strand of hair in rhythm, then you cross your arms in reply. If she says "I hear what you're saying," respond with something like, "Sounds okay to me." If her eyes go over and to the left, send yours down and left as you speak. Get creative. Avoid mimicry.

Once you've achieved some comfort with the components, it will be time to forge communication at the level which people use to advertise *how* they put their world together in their habitual responses.

The added benefit for you to practice comes from helping direct your mind to building up the use of sensory systems you have utilized less frequently until now. If the neurophysiologists are correct, you can actually add to the complexity and efficiency of those portions of your neurological matter by exercising different preferences. Additionally, you will have daily practice interacting with real live people in a fashion different from how you've practiced in the past, but in ways which may serve you well the next time the world dumps a large portion of that sensory-biased experience in your lap—despite the fact that your favorite has always been a different flavor.

o   o   o

Once you are fairly comfortable with each indicator of each system, it is time to respond in kind again. But, this time, instead of just following an eye movement, or a phrase alone, do a bit more. When you have determined a person's preference, which you can discover easily within just a few week's practice, then respond to him with an *unscrambled* delivery. When you start your conversation, go through your new greeting, and then observe his preference. Within a very short time, you will be identifying preferences right away.

At that time, begin your next statement or question by modeling for this person an eye movement, a phrase *and* a gesture associated just with that system. If it turns out to be a lengthy conversation, do this several times. If you bear in mind that most communication is nonverbal, and the vast majority of the mind's functioning is advertised that way, unavailable to conscious discussion, you can appreciate how this is one of the most profound means available to us to approach someone a bit closer to *his* reference for the world. You can communicate with anybody showing respect for the sensory material he has built most of his habitual responses from. It requires no extra vocabulary, time or understanding on your part than you ever used before. Think of the benefits of respecting other people's sensory structures. You get to practice building new habits at the most basic sensory level. People will perceive you as someone not only fully attentive to them, but someone who sees, hears or feels the world the way they do. With practice, the whole process takes less than a couple of minutes. Nobody loses—everybody wins. Most valuable of all, you'll be encouraging the rise of more and more productive sensations in both your engine as well as in the one which pulls the other person's train.

Imagine the salesperson who not only substitutes the customer's feature and benefit words for her own, but also builds a picture for that customer at the same time, gesturing at the view she knows the customer has in his own mind, and remarking how this or that will look, as they both look at this invisible, but highly evocative scene.

Consider the manager, who hands his problem marketer a multi-point list, and then, bobbing his head in time with the marketer's drumming fingers, tells him point-by-point how to say which words in response to which questions, all the while looking side-to-side, then asking if the marketer has anything else to say.

Or how would you feel being the parent or teacher reaching to hold the shoulder of the child who can't quite grasp the idea until you sigh, look down and right, and move the kid's hands through the motions of your explanation, giving each point a physical reference until you feel her excitement transmitted through that touch?

You will be demonstrating back for people a little more of

how they operate more clearly than they do. Almost everybody scrambles the signals instead of straightening them out as you are doing. And when you get in front of a group of people representing different preferences, won't it be grand to make each point along the way, while aligning all three indicators—one after the other?

That's what an attorney friend of mine did when he had a weak case, but a strong conviction that his clients needed his help. He remembered that the meaning of communication is the response of the mind *receiving* that communication. He knew that those minds have practiced biasing themselves along sensory lines for a lifetime and weren't likely to abandon it on account of his own practice of developing a favorite flavor for his own world.

So, when he picked his jurors, he made sure there was one strongly biased toward the auditory, another just as strongly biased toward the visual, and a third who preferred feelings. He delivered his case as well as he could, but his hope lay in the delivery of his closing argument.

Not surprisingly, it was not a recitation of the facts, but a story the attorney used with the jurors—a story which later set a precedent on review in the state court of appeal. Knowing that the most evocative and effective world is one in which all three systems are most fully available and respected, he delivered his story first to one juror, then to the next, and finally to the third of his carefully selected "thermometers".

He realized that the beauty of this approach to communication lies in dumping the notion of communication-as-marksmanship—where a person loads up his message, aims and fires. He knew that since the receiver determines the messages, the more attentive the sender is to the receiver, the more compelling the message will be.

Until the person who liked pictures was nodding in time with his speech as he drew pictures in the air with his eyes upcast, using visual language, he didn't move on. He waited during the next section of the story—or the next point—for the person who liked words and sounds to follow his every move as he used verbal language while keeping time with his foot and moving his eyes only to the left or right whenever they left the face of his listener. Finally, he waited until the person who "felt" his way through the world was in tears before he stopped attracting him with his eyes.

His clients were more than pleased. He had done what even his own partner warned him he could never accomplish. And he did it by relying on communication at its most fundamental: without the words.

o   o   o

The next step beyond greeting a person is to package your message in the most brain-friendly fashion for the receiver by demonstrating respect for his "preferred thinking" sensory system.

11

You Say Yes, I Say No

The engine of sensation is the cue for each and every emotional, mental and behavioral habit we use. A major portion of that sensation is prompted by interactions with people. Those interactions are made up of one part words for every nine parts of nonverbal communication.

By now you know how to practice responding to the behavioral habits of people—which are like personal signatures. You can do this without actually speaking to the person. From that point you can actually greet her and get acknowledged by her mind without her consciously realizing that she has acknowledged you. You can go one step further and register your communication to her within the sensory system she advertises as her favorite one. But how do you know if your well-crafted and politely delivered message actually gets across? How did the attorney introduced earlier know when his opponent was likely to increase his monetary offer, when he affirmed stolidly that he had absolutely no intentions of enlarging the amount?

If the attorney in question had acted as we are encouraged to act by the pundits, he would have had to rely on his own perceptions of what his opponent was really thinking, ignoring the communication entirely.

The perceptions we have been encouraged to trust are characterized by expressions like:

Trusting your feelings; going with your gut reaction;

Flying by the seat of your pants; having a hunch;

Having an intuition; or relying on your own experience.

Habitually, we trust our own sensations regarding the value and accuracy of somebody's communication. We are pulled by the sensation, we react according to old habits, then we use words to justify that response: "Oh, I know it would have been a great deal for me, and I know I lost my house by not buying in, but I always go with *my* feeling when I'm making a big decision."

The attorney learned that if he paid as much attention to the other person's advertising as he did to justify his own impressions about him, he would profit from the investment of his time in direct proportion to the attention he paid out.

This brings us to the next exercise. It requires the taping of a television talk show. Pick one in which incoming calls are taken on the air from people watching at home. Review only a few minutes of the tape at a time. You are looking for phone-in questions which require a "yes" or "no" answer. The speaker will probably elaborate, but find moments when she answers "yes" or "no" at first, and then proceeds to explain her response.

Use more than one example. Record several programs in order to get a fair sampling of behaviors for you to examine.

As the question is asked, even before the person answers, pay attention to what she is *doing*. For the moment, forget about the eye movements and other sensory system indicators. You are looking for something much more basic and easier to discern: It is the fact that people almost always answer the question nonverbally before they answer it out loud.

Watch the woman's head. Watch her eyes. How wide or narrowed are they? Watch her eyebrows, her hands. Observe the way she moves, or tilts her head. Listen to her tone of voice, the pauses and the volume. Draw correlations between "yes" versus "no" answers. Take your time.

In hypnosis and neuroscience, there is a well known phenomenon among human primates called "ideomotor response." This refers to a reflexive form of responsiveness. When used in old-fashioned modes of hypnosis, the operator was required to identify out loud which ideomotor response is requested for which answer. The outdated method consisted of the client holding up an index finger—once she had closed her eyes—and telling her to raise the finger for a 'yes' answer. The little finger was held up indicate a 'no' answer and holding up the middle finger conveyed the response 'I don't care to answer.'

Unfortunately, this method pollutes the natural response outside consciousness with conscious awareness. That won't do. You want a signal or two that remains completely outside the conscious reach of the one with whom you are communicating.

Remember that being creatures of habit, we will never consciously be aware of more than a tiny bit of the ongoing process of our mind's functioning. But to have some conscious sensitivity to *all* the communication of the people around us is necessary. People are, as William Saroyan once said, "... all everything is; all it ever has been, and all it ever will be."

Wouldn't you like to have an ideomotor signaling system set up for the people you live and work with, so that you know your communication efforts have reached them?

Well, you can have that system. As a matter of fact it has been available all along, but people in our culture have been sold so long and hard on the idea that what is in *my* head alone makes all the difference, that we've ignored it.

Check your observations of the people answering questions from unseen questioners such as TV hosts speaking to listeners in their living rooms. Were you able to pick out at least two different ways each person indicated a "yes" response and at least two ways that person indicated a "no" response, even before they answered?

People come with their own built-in ideomotor responses due to years of rehearsal. I trust you discovered by observing the tapes that these responses are *consistent* over time. If somebody nods and raises her tone of voice for a "yes" or agreement, she will do it every time! And she doesn't require a hypnotist to manually wiggle her head up and down for her to learn it. She learned this habit, like all her others from mommy, daddy, the rabbi, television, and so on.

If you haven't yet observed at least two consistent indicators of "yes" and "no" on the tapes you recorded, go back over them again—it is all there. Each person gives away his indicators to anybody willing to climb out of his own head long enough to pay attention to someone else's advertising.

Make a list of ten questions that can be answered unequivocally with a "yes" or "no." "Is your name Jim?" Use simple questions: place of business, job title, home state, home city, dog's name, and so on.

Sit in front of a mirror or your video camera and ask yourself those questions out loud. Watch yourself as you ask and reply. Although it will be challenging to pick out your own responses to questions you already know, rest assured the responses are there. You've practiced these reactions to every "yes" and "no" question for years and years. Stage fright or self-consciousness will not eliminate them.

If you can get two friends to help, here is what you do. Ask one friend a series of "yes" and "no" questions. Be sure they are simple, obvious "yes" and "no" answers. Do you live in an apartment? Is your name Fred? Is that with two ds? Are you an accountant? Avoid any ambiguity, or questions which require a value judgement, like, "Are you having fun?" or, "Do you like your life?".

Have your other friend stop you anytime you move your body or voice in such a way that could be interpreted as "leading the witness" to follow that behavior. If you are not aware of this "leading," you may end up reading your own advertising reflected back at you as the other person's actual response.

Start asking questions and pay close attention to responses. Find at least two or three consistent ways the person indicates a "yes" or "no" reply. Don't say out loud what you believe the indicators to be, rather compare notes with the third party who has been observing as well, and check to see if what you thought you saw and heard was correct. If both of you have noticed different things, go back and continue the questions until each of you has at least the same two consistent indicators of "yes" or "no" without any "leading of the witness."

You don't have to extinguish all of your natural movements and tonal fluctuations for the entire course of a conversation. You don't need to do it at all with people from whom you don't need vital information. But it is important to familiarize yourself with your own habits associated with asking and answering "yes" and "no" questions, if you wish to recognize and relate to people's built-in responses. Without knowing how your eyebrows perform every time you ask a question, how you shake your head only to the right for "no," nod it twice for "yes," or if you are unaware that your voice trails up for every "yes" answer and down for every "no," then you can never trust somebody else's nonverbal responses. Can you guess why?

It has to do with mirroring which we discussed earlier. Don't fool yourself. Everything mentioned in this book has been going on throughout your life. There is nothing in here you can "do" to someone else that isn't being "done" with you all the time.

There is an advantage to practicing awareness and directing those parts of your habits which you have been encouraged to leave on automatic pilot all your life.

If you wish to receive unpolluted answers from somebody—as my attorney friends say—"it's real smart not to lead the witness." Almost every human being —whether she sells used cars or bubblegum machines—has the tendency to lead the answer to questions in the direction of the response she *hopes* to get. And since leading the question falls under communication, 93 percent of it comes in the form of gestures and tones of voice, rather than just shouting, "I want you to say Yes now!" Believe it or not, there are even a few wags out there teaching people to say and do that too!

Gather some friends around to help you discover what your own "yes" and "no" signals are. Keep your poker-playing buddies out of this exercise. You don't want them to know you too well!

I once stood outside a circle of nine people playing poker and watched the goings-on. By the time three hands were played, I was able to tell nine out of ten times—just from facial expressions and tones of voice—which player held a good hand, a bad hand, and who was bluffing, as long as each had held those varieties of hands.

If I was not certain I had spotted the signals correctly, I could speculate about each hand out loud, and the players could not avoid answering even if they said nothing at all. Professional players attempt that trick all the time during a game, which is why chit-chat is not welcome in high stakes poker.

It all depends on your ability to handle yourself the way my attorney friend, Ross, did whenever he asked the opposing counsel if his last offer was truly the final one. Ross knew how to keep silent when his opponent's words didn't match the advertising his opponent's body displayed. If you have ever been confused by mixed messages, this is the cure.

The attorneys I work with have found this skill useful for everything from deposing witnesses, to jury selection. Therapists who practice this routinely use this method for diagnosis. Salespeople make use of it to discover how soon a customer is ready to buy from the part of his mind that *acts,* as opposed to the one that just talks. Managers use it to make certain their communication is getting to across to their co-workers. People tell me they have found it valuable in reassuring themselves that their messages are received as intended in their personal relationships.

But as in most everything that is valuable in human interactions, the key is avoiding "leading the witness" verbally and nonverbally. Most people object to have their sentences finished or have someone speak for them in answer to a question. Nonverbally most of us go one step further and *supply* the answer *during* the question.

Once you are adept at holding your movements and voice fluctuations in check, you can practice anywhere. Whenever you ask for directions or for a suggestion to items on a dinner menu, or ask someone's name, you can practice identifying signals in the person responding. To be certain you aren't fooling yourself, make sure that the questions you ask are very simple.

To make it easier to discern exactly how somebody has

responded, feed back everything she does as she is answering your question. You will have an easier time picking out the things you've just replayed yourself, using your built-in talent for responding in kind. Avoid repeating every word, but pay attention to the tone of her voice.

The system is just as simple as the greeting:

1. Relax completely, and ask a few innocuous questions.
2. Notice and feed back her response.
3. Pick two consistent "yes" and "no" indicators.

When you need to know whether messages are backed by more than just this person's Pez dispenser and caboose, *relax* and pay attention to the responses. Disregard your wishful thinking and avoid "leading the witness."

If you discover that in one situation a person's words say one thing, but everything else tells you differently, you will find yourself in the same position as Ross, with one exception. The opposing attorney was conscious that his answers were not totally forthcoming.

More than once, I have made a business agreement with someone and at a later date asked him to confirm our agreement. I said something like: "So, by February 13th, three things will have been done as specified?"

Although the person is conscious only of the sincere "commitment," "desire," "goal," "objective," "target" or some such nifty-sounding *Active Ingredient*, the rest of his body tells me not to count on our deal coming to pass. He only *thinks* he is going to follow through.

I would be crazy at that point to jump up and shout, "Your head tilted and your voice tone told me you just lied to me!" Of course he didn't. The signals told me at both levels of communication what was most likely. At that point, I don't have a truth detector. But I do have some very valuable information upon which I can plan for the future.

And so will you if you respond in kind to all people, greet some of them at both levels, meet them in their model of the sensory world, and pay closer attention to what they are advertising to you when you let them answer your questions completely.

o   o   o

People advertise their biases in all of their communications, regardless of what they may say in words.

*"Don't aim at success—
the more you aim at it and make it a target,
the more you are going to miss—
it must ensue as the unintended side effect
of one's personal dedication to
a course greater than himself."*
Victor Frankl

12

Deadlines and Starting Lines: Brain-Friendly Instructions and Goals

Now that you understand the basics for interactions which respect people's minds, here are a few suggestions on how to utilize brain-friendly approaches in two of the most common situations: *giving instructions and setting goals.*

The common denominator for instructions and goals is the association your mind makes with "creativity." When creativity comes into play, it can either be a hindrance or an advantage. When you have given someone precise instructions on how to handle a project or situation, the last thing you want is for that person to "get creative." But when you have set goals, it is your creativity that will lead you to the required results.

Instructions

A phrase most commonly heard in the offices of family therapists, divorce lawyers, office managers and business consultants is:

"We have a communication problem."

Often, the problems have to do with getting an instruction safely from one person's head to the person who has to act on the instruction, in some form close to the original intention..

Being aware of the nature of the mind when you are giving instructions alleviates big problems. The following is a useful pattern:

1. Greet people, meet their sensory bias, and pay attention to their "yes" and "no" response habits.

2. Keep their attention while delivering your instructions in their favorite sensory system—checking for agreement periodically

3. Tailor your instructions to be specific about the *standard and manner* you wish the job to be done. Avoid *negatives and abstractions.*

Keeping Attention

When you are instructing someone on how, when and where to do a job, check in on him periodically as you go. It is important to go through the process of greeting the individual again. You would be surprised how often someone who you thought was paying attention to you was really lost in her head and only appeared to hear you. When it comes to passing on specific instructions, particularly if you're not going to be around while the work is being carried out, assure yourself that you have the full attention of the listener.

Sensory Packaging

What may be "perfect" instructions inside your head become upside-down, backwards and topsy-turvy messages by the time they arrive in someone else's head. That's because we usually give instructions which are "perfect" for ourselves only. Deliver your instructions within a package of gestures, phrases and eye movements appropriate to the system which the recipient of your message prefers.

Your job as a teacher, manager, parent or partner requires that you give clear, precise instructions. It may be obvious, but you have no idea how many clients and organizations have told me about the following disappointment:

Ms. Manager gave Ms. Employee a list of seven things to do six weeks ago Tuesday. Ms. Manager insists she gave instructions in clear direct terms—her instructions were "Perfect. Absolutely perfect in every way."

The only problem was that Ms. Employee delivered the assignment two days late, upside-down and backwards. She explains, "I did it exactly the way she told me to do it...exactly!"

It was not just the employee's fault. True, she didn't know how to ask adequate questions. On the other hand, it was Ms. Manager's responsibility to deliver her instructions in a manner the employee could use.

Checking Agreement

Taking a person's word that he "understands" your instructions means that he is only seven percent sure of delivering the task as directed. Relying on his nonverbal agreement and disagreement signals is far more productive.

Let's say you are announcing four chores that Binky has to do this weekend if he wants to go to the concert next Saturday. As you recite the four points, summarize them and avoid leading the witness, then make sure his mind has grasped the information at each point.

The same principle applies at work with two additions. First, it helps to pay attention to what comes out of the person's mouth as you check for agreement point-by-point. He may be telling you what short-cuts he knows, or what pitfalls he foresees. Secondly, professionals have a tendency to give long and complicated instructions. In that case check for nonverbal agreement as you go over each point, and *again* at the end of the summary. If you notice some ambivalence in his reaction to a specific point, address it immediately. It is not necessary to tell him consciously what prompted you to reiterate the point. Leave what is outside consciousness right where it is, but by all means show some respect for it.

If you get an unsatisfactory response when you have come to the end of the list, and you don't know which one of the points the response refers to, go back over the list while "thinking out loud." Carefully watch out of the corner of your eyes for a response. If he agrees with each point, question him briefly about what he thinks of the project as a whole—and not of the particular points.

Remember to place the *Reactive Role* on yourself. "Confess" to some misgivings or discomfort about the priority of the task at hand. Often, the part of the mind which balked will speak right up if you invite him to do so in this gentle fashion. Often, people won't have had any conscious awareness that they even had objections or second thoughts until you invite them to consider the idea, even though they cued you to do so.

Standard and Manner

Be sure you use specific language when discussing the *Standard* and *Manner* in which you wish a certain task to be done.

Standard refers to the limits you are placing on the instructions for the task. Be specific about the exact time you wish a job done. What color paper do you want to be used? Do you ask for progress reports along the way? How should mistakes or questions be handled? What if something else comes up? Limits of resources, time, outlays, interruptions, intervening priorities, questions, unforeseen circumstances need to be specified in your language. To suggest, "Use your best judgment"—won't cut it.

Manner refers to the way you want the job done. Again, your language best be simple and direct and as specific as possible. How many hours do you want spent on the job during the day? Can she take it home? Can Bobby help her? Can she change the title if she comes up with a "better" one? Who gets to know about it? How much can she spend? Does she have to clear expenditures with anyone? Does she need to coordinate with anyone? If so, how often and in what form will coordination take place? How will she know when she is finished? Can she leave anything out? And so on.

If you ask someone to do something and you are not specific about the *Standard* and *Manner* in which the chore is to be executed, you have no right to complain about the results. If you lack being specific, then you will get only what the receiver perceived you were asking. If instructions are complex, then writing down the specific *Standard* and *Manner* eliminates repeating the instructions when the person asks yet another question: "What did you mean about...?"

Giving instructions is one of the few times when concentrating on the words can actually be helpful in communication. By specifying behaviors which fully address the *Standard* and *Manner* the task requires, you help control the creativity of the individual's mind to stray and to steer clear of generalized labels from which he can draw his own behavioral conclusions.

Keep in the front of your mind the fact that what is crystal clear to you is as clear as mud to your audience. For example, imagine sitting at your desk, with your back half-turned away from the person you're speaking with, as you look at the progress chart on the wall behind you.

You say, "We're coming up to the end of the quarter, as you can see. We need those printed materials corrected and re-done as soon as possible. Can I rely on you to make that your number one priority? We have a presentation due next week, and I don't want to go empty-handed. Do you know what I mean?"

Absent in the message were clear instructions for the time of delivery. It *could* be next week, or it *could* be the end of the quarter. Won't you be surprised when this individual, following your instructions, drops everything in preparation for *his* part in next week's presentation because he perceived his job to be following the printed materials by hand through to completion?

If you had turned to face him at the start, assured yourself that you had all of his attention, then you might have pointed at the chart on the wall to focus his attention.

You could then have had definite agreement signals about the *Standard* and *Manner* of the job: what day and time the project was to be delivered and what specific behaviors the person associated with priority jobs. If you failed to attend to how your instructions were being taken, you received exactly what you instructed him to bring to you.

Negatives

Any time you deliver an instruction in a negative form, you're asking for trouble. The mind works on experience, not reasons. It will almost always complicate matters if you describe what you *do not* want done, what you *never* want done again, or what *can't* ever happen again.

Disciplining children with these admonitions is a terrific way to put children and parents into the streets waving their arms and foaming at the mouth. It works only slightly less dramatically at work.

If someone makes a mistake and it can be corrected easily, be cautious about fixing it with a "This was wrong—this is right" delivery. This is the true reason behind the downfall of managers who rely on threats of dismissal to direct an employee's performance. If you are perceived by that person as the *Active Party,* as you do the criticizing you are inviting him to connect you and your accusation with all the other "wrong" sensations in his body. And in his mind, your face will become a reminder of that unproductive feeling.

Some use the same judgmental implications to instruct people how to do something new and different—which by its very nature has not been around long enough to be judged "wrong." After all, how "wrong" could someone be for *not* doing something he has not been asked to do as yet? But how often have you heard words such as, "Damn, how could something that important not have been done? Somebody should have realized we'd be needing this gidget by now. Am I the only one thinking around here?"

In family situations you hear the very same judgmental implications in the whining of teenagers, "Why didn't you tell me that before now?" Parents are not exempt. They often slip up with comments to youngsters such as, "Well, you should have known, anyway. I didn't raise an idiot, did I? Where was your head?".

Negative judgments come up between couples, who, when one is trying to instruct the other on how he would appreciate more affectionate gestures, drop bombs on the unsuspecting mind of his partner like: "[Sigh]—It's okay. I just wish you'd done things differently. It sure would have been nice if you..."

Lots of instructions *are* designed to "fix" unproductive actions, habits or trends. But even instructions aimed at developing new and different trends and behavior deserve to be delivered free of negative implications. Watch your language and the messages they carry between the lines, to be sure you clearly imply what you *want* to get across.

Abstractions

You know about labels and their inadequacies as effective communicators particularly in guiding someone's actions in real life. No matter how evocative you may find certain labels to be, definitions like *Entrepreneurial Spirit, True Commitment* or *Unconditional Anything* never come across as intended. People can't divine the story which resides between your ears from phrases like, "What I want from you is a much more aggressive tolerance in delegating."

If you expect people to use your abstract expressions as a guide for future behavior, advise them to leave a trail of bread crumbs when they go, or you'll never find them again.

Goals

Goals are different from instructions. Though both deal with future behavior that will have to be accomplished along certain lines, instructions have the benefit of being specific. Goals are one part hope and one part mystery. Goals rarely work out exactly the way they are planned because life is like that.

That does not mean that some of the things you have learned to apply to instructions don't apply equally well to goal-setting. If you are among the frustrated individuals who persist in setting goals for themselves or others which require accomplishing a negative abstraction, you may now stop. If you talk about a goal in a negative manner, don't be surprised when exactly what you want to avoid shows up on your doorstep. The mind works on experience; it doesn't quite understand "No."

This happens specifically when it comes to setting a goal for something we want to correct or avoid. Imagine you are the proud parent of an adolescent girl, and that she has a bigger form than the currently ideal shape for adolescent girls—which often resembles a small, pre-pubescent boy. If you are tempted to tell your child: "Honey, don't you think you're getting too heavy? Don't you think it would be a good idea for you to not carry so much weight? You don't want to feel ugly, do you?" —please, stop and think again.

Do you hear the implications in these judgment-laden phrases? Negative-charged instructions are like *"Failure Preparation."* Pay attention to the sensory nature of your goals. If you set goals for others, the same rule as for instructions applies. Set the goal in the system the person prefers. If you are setting goals for yourself, be a bit more adventurous and represent your end results in all three systems. Picture yourself there as you feel the thrill of hearing you've made your goal.

And, like giving instructions, if you are helping somebody set goals for work or play and you don't check with her outside consciousness to discover whether or not that part of her agrees, then plan for a disappointment.

Avoid negatives, respect sensory preferences and, whenever possible, check for agreement nonverbally. That is where the similarities between instructions and goal setting end.

There is only one basic guideline to follow when setting behavioral goals:

Set General Directions and Save the Specifics for the Trip.

When it comes to personal performance, the more specific your goals, the more limited you become.

That may be a departure from conventional dogma, but so is the idea that consumers need protection for their minds. It makes perfect sense if you consider what you are asking your mind to do: receive instructions and set goals.

With instructions, you use specific language to zero in on the desired behavior, limiting creativity. Following instructions is all about paying attention to the limits on your behavior, not exploring various options. Goals require the exact opposite approach to the way the mind works. When you are aiming at new habits for your thinking and actions in a certain time or place, the last thing you want to do is limit your options for success. Specifically defining exactly "how, when, where, what and how much" only serves to deprive your mind of anything but the most minor portion of its resources—your conscious labels. Creativity is not a conscious process. Trying to specifically predict the outcome by managing creativity consciously is like trying to plan spontaneity.

On the other hand, goals can drift too easily into the land of generalizations and labels and become impotent. Today, people frequently fall prey to making firm "commitments." In days past, people announced their good "intentions." And, using the same habit of substituting a word for an action as children, we all indicated loudly how hard we were going to "try" to do something. The less we expected to succeed, the more we declared our "trying."

All too many people are seduced by the power of language to distract our conscious attention from reality to a fantasy "vision" of how well everything is going to be once we make a "commitment." Not realizing the difference outside consciousness, our minds conjure up the sense of those imagined experiences. We associate with the images and feel as if we had actually taken some action.

Affirmations, Guided Imagery, Creative Visualization, Peak Performance Conditioning and a dozen other plans owe their popularity to the public's recognition of the fact that the mind plays a role in determining our success. However, any approach which insists on a constant string of specific verbalizations and images being repeated like mantras in your head is limiting in two different ways:

First, your excitement about the project you are planning can actually be weakened by this concentrated mind-game, leaving you with little energy to start the actual work. You delay. The mind doesn't form new habits from intentions— no matter how serious or exciting they may momentarily seem.

Second, mental repetition before the fact actually limits your creativity. By concentrating on exactly how you want to do something, exactly when it will occur, and specifically what every step will be, you insure that only those features of your stored experience which are *already* available to you in consciousness will be reinforced. You are trying to build something new, with *old* tools. Einstein said, "You can't solve a problem using the same thinking that created it."

Starting Lines—not Finishes

You may be wondering what I mean exactly by setting a general direction for goals, but not being too specific about the results at the same time.

The point of a goal is just that: to point your mind in a specific direction. The idea is not to eliminate possible alternatives to moving in that direction. It is a challenge, but rewarding to quit pretending we can predict exactly how we will achieve success. When people are involved, we cannot control the process or predict the course of events with accuracy.

A woman named Rose who had attended one of my classes returned to another seminar to debate the value of starting lines versus finish lines as goals. She had used visualized affirmations in the past to see herself successfully participating in a singing recital she was rehearsing.

Rose had a strong affinity for the visual and auditory portions of her experience, but she consciously leaned toward the pictures. She had creatively visualized every part of this concert, "...The shoes I have on, the faces of the audience, the sounds I'm making...I am singing better than I ever have..." She affirmed herself fifteen minutes before each rehearsal and fifteen minutes after. And in front of my class she replayed the whole story.

Standing in front of her, I formed an imaginary "screen" with my hands superimposed on the spot she had already been picturing herself. I said, "Let me get this straight. You imagined what you would be wearing, how everything looked, sounded and felt like. You imagined before and after each rehearsal singing 'better that you ever had before,' and when the time came you did just that. Is that correct?" She nodded, "Yes, I sang better than I ever had, exactly as I planned."

"Pity," I replied.

At that point I took the imaginary screen from three feet in front of her at eye level, and began backing up with it, slowly turning to the left,until the screen (my hands) was sideways to her and all she could see was the side of my left hand. As I moved, I said, "It's a pity that you proved your mind works, but used the process to limit yourself. What you didn't know was that down the road and around this corner (I had now turned my hands) was something a *thousand times more* beautiful than you could ever have consciously imagined."

I then quickly brought the "screen" back to its original position in front of her face and concluded, "But you insisted on improving only as much as you could *consciously* imagine. That's a pity."

Rather than succumb to the simple, easy solution habit of thinking which advertises absolute control of the future for anyone who is able to specify her goals sufficiently, I use brief, general terms to set my directions so my conscious attention is least distracted from the task at hand by brilliant fantasy. After all, I will never get to my goal if my efforts are constantly diluted by elaborate wishful thinking.

Brain-friendly performance goals come in two forms—brief and general. Professionally, quantitative measures like fifty more sales contacts per month, or $10,000 more in sales per quarter are fine, as long as you avoid sitting at your desk imagining exactly what it will be like to have achieved your new goals and exactly how you will accomplish them, while the time ticks rapidly away. Having meetings to detail these fantasies is equally counter-productive. Voting on the top three is a complete waste of time. On the other hand, getting real-work input from colleagues *as you travel* can be valuable, indeed.

Abstract language helps to keep your mind on track—not the unknown destination five miles down a track you've *never* travelled. Say something to yourself like, "I wonder how well I'll be doing, feeling, handling this, soon." Sigh just before closing your eyes then open them and refocus on the world. You will be much more likely to remember at once to bring your attention back into the people around you. You will accomplish what you set out to do without dictating to your mind how to do the part of the job that *it* is expert at. After all, if you were conscious of precisely how to reach this goal, wouldn't you have already done it?

Remember how vast the resources of your mind outside consciousness are. How can you presume to tell your mind how much of which stored experience to use? Faust is a good example of someone who had a terrible time specifying what he thought it was that he wanted, when he actually was confronted with having his wishes granted.

I was once told that people have a tendency to live both up and down to their expectations of themselves. When we set goals in a consciously limited, verbally specific fashion, we will always run the risk of living down to our expectations. When it comes to improving our behavior, it is much more in tune with the mind's functioning to set a general direction and use it like a compass.

Our conscious energy and attention can then be used to insure that we are really travelling in that direction. That frees us to attend to unexpected pitfalls along the way. We will discover all kinds of new and useful things, as well as our fellow travelers whom we would have missed by concentrating on a tunnel-vision image of what we imagined the end of the road would be.

o   o   o

Complementary, but opposite rules apply. The common bottom line is behavior, which is generated from direction (experience) more than from dictation (speech). The big difference is that with instructions specificity eliminates confusion, while with performance goals it limits creativity.

13

Your Train of Thought: Use It or Lose It

By now you should feel more comfortable with your *Train of Thought and Action.* You know the engine represents that sensation along your midline—comfortable or otherwise—which prompts your habitual reactions. These reactions are the cars you have built to carry you safely and successfully through the situations life presents. And there's the caboose, where—having already reacted—you can find the words to discuss your moods, your biases in thinking, and your habitual actions. There's only the engineer missing.

Only the engineer can steer your train. Each moment in your life—especially those moments of interactions with people—provide you with opportunities to steer down the same old track you've always followed, or down a completely new one—if you notice the chances and know the way to go.

Your conscious awareness is your engineer. You can only

redirect your habits of thinking and acting by consciously taking note of the time when it is beneficial to go down a different track. It is only by attending consciously to what's going on around you, how well or poorly your efforts are met by the real world, that you have a chance to switch tracks and derail some old, unproductive habits.

The conscious mind, the engineer, can only do one thing at a time. If your engineer is lounging in the caboose philosophizing about life's troubles and blaming last year's simple solution for this year's complicated problems, then nobody is steering your train. You can either spend your time commenting on the situation or attending to the results you are actually getting—right now. You cannot do both at once. And, as you know, *talk always follows actions.*

It is necessary to give all that up in order to build the most effective working relationship possible for using both the conscious and other-than-conscious parts of your mind. It is an illusion that we can control the process and predict the outcomes of our efforts in human situations. What remains is to discard the habit of seeking answers to "why," and to concentrate on "when" would be a good time to jump the tracks and head in a different direction.

The words you speak are never as real to someone else as they are to you. Language is not objective—it is completely subjective. Our "common language" is anything *but* common. It influences us, but it won't create new habits, only reinforce old ones by pointing your train along the lines of your conscious, verbal musings.

We know that the associations we've built in our minds from our accumulated experiences influence our habits of thinking toward some responses and away from others. Habits of thinking combine with our behavioral habits to form the patterns and reactions people recognize as our personality.

Finally, we know that the force which provides the energy to drive our train down the tracks—every mile, every day—is provided by the feelings from which we react. Our senses pick up experiences in the moment and are processed by our minds outside of conscious scrutiny and send us comfortable or uncomfortable sensations which cue our habitual responses.

By now, you have been practicing several new ways of reacting to words, thinking habits, reaction patterns and the sensations that drive them. By practicing the methods in this book, you are guaranteed to experience a slightly awkward sensation which will soon become a habitual cue for you to sigh— interrupting your accustomed responses.

At this point you can elect to do something different than you have done in the past, especially if you don't wait to tell yourself out loud or in your head what that different something is going to be. Do the most brain-friendly thing of all and concentrate your conscious attention more on the productive interaction between you and another person, rather than on your thoughts about yourself.

Instead of creating a conflict over whose version of a word is right, or whose conscious recall of a past event is correct, remember that everybody has a different "ocean" in his head. Set the conflict aside. Avoid capitulating, just put first things first and use the conflict as a reminder to *greet, meet and assure* yourself and the other person that you are giving him your full attention.

Remember that every interaction offers you chances to put each one of the exercises—or starting lines—in this book into play for yourself and those around you. Please practice only one—or one part—of each exercise at a time. Avoid overburdening your engineer.

Using TV Without It Using You

Television is a fact of life today, and no matter how much people may complain about it, it is not going away. The number of hours adults spend in front of the tube every week is rising, and younger viewers are spending more hours than ever watching television programs.

I propose that we put television to better use than we ever imagined we could. We can actually practice our skills for interacting with people more productively while watching the small screen and still enjoy the programs.

You know now that the mind absorbs and reacts more to implications than intentions. In order to understand the images and words it receives, the mind must represent them as experience behind the scene of consciousness. If for example, you see a dead body on the six o'clock news for the usual visual bite of twenty seconds, your mind is referencing the images and words you hear and see as if they were real events in your inner experience.

Imagine what happens to that inner experience, when, one second later, the scene in front of you changes and you are looking at a miraculous one-handed catch by a wide-receiver of the football team for a big win. Your mind makes absolutely no distinction between the relative *value* you might place on each of two events if you were to stop and discuss them consciously. You are constantly rehearsing what you reference at the rate of thousands of bits of information per second, long before you can talk about it.

The average 18-year old adult in our country has witnessed over 10,000 homicides by graduation day. Some of the murder scenes were immediately followed by pictures of a young woman in a brief bikini, draped over shiny new automobile she is pitching for the manufacturer. Can you imagine what our minds have been invited to do? Does this give substance to the people who voice worries about our loss of respect for each other? Imagine how blunted the impact of an ordinary emotional wound becomes after we have mentally rehearsed responding to viewing our nine-thousandth murder. Imagine in what kind of context that murder is absorbed into our minds when it is followed instantly by a *Cocoa Puffs* commercial.

The overall speed and bizarre sequencing of commercial television cannot help but imply a world in which virtually *anything* becomes nothing more than grist for the mill. On the tube, all human experiences, the loftiest and the lowliest, are guaranteed two things—it won't last long, and it won't end up meaning much more than the next commercial, as far as your mind is concerned. Everything becomes a detached form of entertainment whether it was intended to be viewed as such or not.

Consider some of the broad-level implications of various forms of TV programming. For instance, what kind of a world is inferred by the half-hour sitcom or the hour-long drama? — one in which any problem has a simple and rapid solution? One which tolerates no ambiguity? One in which there is virtually *always* a predictable, happy ending within the time slot conveniently arranged between commercials?

How about television news? How many sides to an issue are there? Do you ever get more than two views ? And how often are they presented in such a manner that they are not telegraphing which one is "right?" What is the length of the average in-depth analysis of a subject on the evening news? More than two minutes?

What is your mind to make of the relative importance of the ideas, events and lives which can't possibly be examined in two minutes? Is it any wonder that the newly-free Eastern Bloc nations immediately clamored for actions to solve their problems after only a short time under their new governments? After all, it's got to be *Miller Time*—now!

What do you learn by inference about various groups presented on television? Are doctors and lawyers represented as stereotypes in contrast to parents or politicians? How many children are represented as smart by spouting sarcastic remarks at their "parental units" rather than being featured excelling in school? How many captains of industry did you see represented as moral, upright and generous lately ?

Unless we closely watch out for the influences of the sensory "programming" in television, we have no choice but to absorb all of the less-than-stellar images it exposes us to on a minute-to-minute basis.

1. *Active Ingredients*: If there is one social entity which supports and spreads the illusion that there is and should always be one right answer for every human situation, it is television. More than higher education, more than politics, more than the sciences, programs daily spread the doctrine of "Just tell me why" to millions of unprepared minds in hundreds of ways.

After the miracle catch is made, the reporters jam microphones in their faces and ask the football hero, "Exactly what was going through your mind? What were you thinking that enabled you to make that fabulous catch?"

Every newscaster on the scene interviews a "face" which claims to have known the criminal or candidate or victim as a child. The face has the exclusive answer to the inevitable question, "Why do you think she did it?" Talk shows are usually set-ups between two opposing "why-merchants" defending their "right" answer.

2. *Either/Or*: As a result of our reliance on *Active Ingredients* to explain our existence, we frequently end up comparing *two*

different "right" answers about a human condition which is not a puzzle and doesn't need a solution. Because of the implicit judgments that accompany this game, we are invited to make choices between competing labels. The difficulty is that the mind won't stop at the label, but takes all the experiences associated with a specific word and discredits them along with the label. We end up receiving messages which inform us that we must decide between simplified abstracts, which in actuality banish complicated, cultural realities. Then the talking heads ask where our "tolerance" has gone!

When tied to generalizations in language, implications encourage the worst kind of expectations and fears, and they are everywhere. Here are just a few: "Either *they* are ruining our economy or *they* are not. Either *they* want to be helped or *they* don't. Either we take care of *ourselves* or *them. We* can't help *everybody. People* have been allowed to do this for too long—it's either *their* interests, or *our children's.* Are *you* for a good country, or aren't you?"

3. *Outside/In:* This implication is an outgrowth of our attempts to have an answer for everything, and the *answer* is the word. This fosters the illusion of having conscious control over everything from falling in love to falling into depression. The result is a "television world" represented as if virtually *everything* which has an impact on our life comes from "outside" us. We are treated hourly to images of people who are :

Overcome by depressions—swept away by passion—unable to help themselves—waiting for some relief—loving what Toyota does for me—healthier, happier, smarter, sexier, more fulfilled, wealthier, more powerful, more accepted, and more respected because they bought, picked up, acquired, surrendered to, finally reached, invested in, realized, purchased, and dealt with some *thing.*

4. *Dissatisfaction*: Two of the biggest purveyors of our dissatisfaction with our existences are television news and commercials. These two powers join forces to make certain that everybody on the other side of the tube is reminded just how inadequate, disgusting, dangerous and even hopeless our lives are. This influence is so pervasive on television that you probably already have examples coming to mind. How often are you informed — by a face and voice on television—that parts of your body could be more acceptable than they are? When was the last time you were reminded how little real value your current possessions have, while there is lots of better stuff available? When was the last time you were told how stupid your children are...how dangerous our streets have become...how little one person can do to change things? And so it goes.

Knowing that the mind works more effectively on implications and impressions than explanations and intentions, the value of turning all the messages between the lines on television to your advantage becomes pretty clear.

Soap operas are wonderful for catching references in connection with *Active Parties*. As you watch and listen, ask yourself something like, "Who's doing what to whom?" You will be amazed how easily you discover when people are being "acted upon" as opposed to "acting on" their worlds.

If you want to notice how careless people are about putting events into proper perspective, watch and listen to talk shows. You will never hear people characterizing their disorders, dysfunctions or social maladies as having happened "in the past, up till now, once a week, or way back then." You will find an almost perverse delight in the hosts and guests implying that whatever ill is being discussed exists—stuck in time—as if it always has and always will be the way it is described now.

If you want some rehearsal for acting "In Body" or "In

Head," watch people reading from a teleprompter or reciting memorized lines for you. You will become familiar with the obvious signs of disassociation from the body which these person's demeanors invite your mind to *practice* all day long. (And people wonder what causes them to have so much trouble with "intimacy.")

Check out the politicians any time you want a refresher course in how suggestions of *possibility* versus *scarcity* work. Also, media analysts, television cops, doctors and lawyers can give you ample rehearsal on noticing when people are implying how much you've got to give up in order to get something (scarcity).

Can you remember the last time you heard a politician who wasn't running for office say something chock full of implied possibilities? No, they're busy telling you why the opposition is depriving you of what you hired *them* to accomplish. Then, try to find one who *is* running for re-election who is not clamoring for time to tell you the unlimited possible benefits if you were to vote for him.

You are probably aware of the metaphors behind the stories you hear on television. Here is just one example to remind you: "We formed a *plan of attack,* and are prepared to *launch* our *assault* with all the *force* at our disposal. I have no doubt we will be *victorious.*" Was the warfare metaphor in this case referring to a sportscast, a newscast, a doctor show or a business drama?

Recognizing judgmental thinking habits only requires five minutes of attentive, random viewing. Take aspirin commercials. There are several products being presented to you which all have exactly the same ingredients. The only way these companies distinguish their products is to sling judgmental implications around about their competitor's product made from the exact same chemicals.

Perhaps some of the more heartbreaking judgmental suggestions are weight-loss commercials, specials and infomercials. By implication, you are first invited to equate your body with your entire self. Then you are told how you can "improve" this *self* of yours by shaving-down its silhouette, while enjoying the process. Do you remember an old slogan from the industry that went, "Lose your*self* in the taste?" Does that seem a bit less innocent when you become aware of the coaching your mind is receiving on its *habits of thinking* between the lines? (Can't they find some aspect of "self" separate from "body?")

There are some just plain silly things implied on commercials which can provide hours of unbridled hilarity. It seems that the sillier the implication, the more frequently it is repeated. One of my all-time favorite sources of mirth was again supplied by the weight-loss industry. This commercial promised you that by paying a flat amount of money, the weight loss company in question will allow you to "Lose all the weight you can."

Think. Even if you were to *gain* weight, all they've promised is to keep your money. Incidentally, this one was so obvious that the company discontinued the commercial..

There are ample opportunities offered on television to practice more productive language habits without diminishing your enjoyment of the medium. Actually, you will probably enjoy it a bit more.

1. Labeling And Active Ingredients: With language it's not enough to just consider which way you want to lean, as it is with implications. Once you appreciate the down side of an implication, the other side has already presented itself in your mind. But, with words substitutions are necessary.

Television is a great label-maker; its survival depends on reducing complexity to verbal simplicity. You won't ever have trouble finding labels—especially the "explanatory" labels or

Active Ingredients. Just apply yourself, and don't be distracted by whatever the words conjure up in your head, long enough to determine whether you want that association reinforced.

Here are a several examples of switching labels:

Remember that when you are distracted by the value attached to the reference for a particular word, you *lose*. It's the person who is most prepared to dump a label (even a long-standing favorite) who will succeed in the real world. Would you rather be "retarded" or "crippled," or would you prefer to be "mentally or physically-challenged?" On the other hand, would you prefer identifying yourself as someone who "abuses alcohol" or as someone who is a "dependency victim?" Are you short of stature, or are you vertically disadvantaged? Each label offers a specific direction for your head.

2. References & Judgment: This is not only about who or what is being placed in the role of *Active Party* by the words, but who or what is in the role of judging what is right or wrong. Practice sharpening this particular tool. It will come in handy in finding language to defuse personal conflicts and to guard against messy politics in the workplace. Things like:

"It would be nice if...", "It's about time for...", "No one knows why...", "The Arabs are in a no-win situation...", "The American people want...", "Real value for your dollar...", "Traditional family values...", "More satisfying than..."

The above examples of language could benefit by revealing *Who* or *What* specifically is in charge. "No-win according to whom" is what you might ask yourself when you hear these disembodied declarations march by on your video screen.

The more judgment implied by a statement, the more likely an Active Party being referenced won't be specified in words. For example, "No way that's right, Fred!" or "How dare she say something like that behind his back?" or "You know about *them,* don't you?" are potent, rabble-rousing remarks. But, according to whose rules is the rabble being roused here? Practice identifying the *Active Party* being referenced, so that you can rephrase the comment whenever *you* want to be the one your mind perceives as acting.

The everyday language of television is filled with chances for us to talk back and clean-up the language we might otherwise unthinkingly rehearse and store. Whenever we hear a talking-head declare a "reason" for a certain action or situation, we can say softly to ourselves, "Or, on the other hand...according to another authority..."

If you hear a salesman tell you to "Say yes to whatever makes your life richer, more fulfilling and powerful, more delightful and rewarding..." then your reply is "According to whom, Buckwheat?" Television offers us constant opportunities to challenge the question "why" when it comes to human behavior.

Television has become the powerful influence on our culture and it offers us golden opportunities to practice interactions, making them "natural", so that when we bump into some real people we will be even more adept in their presence.

For practice interacting, restrict yourself to programs which have live audiences responding spontaneously to the issues at hand rather than having to rely on cue cards or memorized dialogue. Tape a show, and play it back several times until you are sure that you have identified and even counted the various numbers of sense-words and phrases each individual used.

Turn the picture back up and turn the sound down—you can now observe the participants' gestures. Since the camera operators on these shows have practiced these skills on their own, you are being given a virtual *primer* on eye movements every time Phil or Sally or Oprah ask someone a question. If you own a VCR, you can isolate them, access movement until you are comfortable viewing at slow speed, then you can advance the speed of the tape until you can catch the action as it happens. Repeat the process several times.

Within a pretty short time, you can form some educated guesses about the relative strengths of each of the three indicators (phrases, gestures and eye movements) for anyone who is on camera for more than 20 to 30 seconds. You will have a new crop of people to practice with from day to day.

Listen to a live talk show (at home on the radio or in the car) and carefully mimic the tones, rhythms, timbre, breathing and pace used by each speaker. Pretty soon you will be able to copy their phrases—their way—just a word or two behind them. Tape yourself to check your progress more objectively.

Don't forget facial movements, postures and gestures. You can do with television what I would never advocate you do in real life: match everything you can for as long as you wish. Remember that in real life, mirroring even the smallest bits of demeanor doesn't take longer than 30 seconds. With television you can extend the mirroring for as long as you want. Be sure you limit mirroring with the people in your life, or risk acting rudely.

In case you have a video camera, tape yourself matching people on television. Again, you may be surprised by what you thought was a "perfect" match. More important, you will most probably catch yourself in several movements in contrast to what the television personality was demonstrating.

Even without a camera, the more you sensitize yourself to the movements you need to match other people, the more your mind outside consciousness will reveal your everyday, unthinking behaviors to your conscious engineer. You will then have the unique opportunity to thank yourself for pointing out something you may not have noticed you have been doing in conversations with pretty much everybody—probably for years and years. Keep in mind all the other exercises you have already practiced with the help of your television set.

Typically, television is a force which invites us to lessen our interactive capacities, but at the same time it actually could help us in the process. Now, that's entertainment!

Remember that nobody fails alone. Nobody succeeds alone. And happiness is pursued best not by attending to yourself, but to productive interactions with other people.

o o o

A key to a happier, more fulfilled life with others is to keep your attention out of your head and in to your interactions with others.

For information on speaking
engagements and seminars for trial
attorneys or the general public, or
in-house consultations:

call:

800-392-3314
—for scheduling and fees—

or write:

MetaSystems
42015 Ford Road #224
Canton, MI 48187

About The Author

Eric Oliver, founder of MetaSystems, a Michigan-based training and consulting firm has been highly successful with "interventions" as a remarkable technique to help people change the way they think and deal with other people. So effective has Oliver become that much of his work involves advising litigating attorneys on methods to improve their communication with clients and their effectiveness in the courtroom.

A member of the American Society of Trial Consultants, Eric's corporate clients include AT&T, the former Sperry-Univac, Northern States Power, The Minnesota Trial Lawyers Association, Continental Medical Systems, Target Systems International, and representatives of Control Data, GTE, GM, Honeywell, MONY, ReMax, Coldwell Banker, Century 21 and many others.

Eric has appeared many times on television and radio and is the author of *The Human Factor At Work*. He has also written and produced two audiotape programs entitled, *Pursuing Happiness On The Train Of Thought,* and *Consumer Protection For The Mind*. Eric resides with his wife and partner, Tess, in the Detroit, Michigan area.

To Learn More About
The Human Factor At Work

Order Form

	Price	Quantity	Total
The Human Factor At Work	14.95	_____	_____
News From The Mental Edge	16.95	_____	_____
Annual subscription to quarterly			
newsletter.			
Pursuing Happiness On The Train	189.00	_____	_____
Of Thought			
6 Cassettes in a binder			
Consumer Protection For The Mind	39.95	_____	_____
4 Cassettes with workbook			
Shipping/Handling (each item)	3.50	_____	_____
Total Order		_____	_____

Name: _____

Address: _____

City/State/Zip:_____

Phone: Bus.: _____ Home: _____

If paying with credit card, please complete information below:

[ ] Visa [ ] MasterCard

_____ _____/_____ _____
   Card #   Expiration Date   Your Signature

Please return this order form with check or money order payable to:

MetaSystems
42015 Ford Road #224
Canton, MI 48187

TO ORDER TODAY CALL
800-392-3314